MAPPING BALI

ISLAND • CULTURE • PEOPLE

First published in 2023 by

Talisman Publishing Pte Ltd
talisman@apdsing.com
www.talismanpublishing.com

ISBN 978-981-14-5059-4

Publisher
Ian Pringle

Text, and Illustrations
Bruce Granquist

Additonal Illustration Support
Gede Wijaya
Putu Ngurah Yasa
Nengah Nurenten
Mubinas Hanaffi
Natalia Granquist
Mark Hopkins

Design
Talisman Publishing: Stephy Chee & Wong Sze Wey

Studio Manager
Janice Ng

Printed in Singapore

MAPPING BALI

ISLAND • CULTURE • PEOPLE

A Book By

Bruce Granquist

TALISMAN

DEDICATION

This book is dedicated to my family and friends who supported this project, even though it was largely invisible for more than 2 decades. I could have not wished for more loyal support.

Banyualit
Kalibubuk
Kaliasem
Gambuh
Munduk Kunci
Jembong
Pegayaman
Gitgit
Selat
Labuanaji
Temukus
Kayuputih Melaka
Sinalud
Kalianget
Dencarik
Melanting
Tampekan
Banjar
Tigawasa
Panti
Yeh Ketipat
Lemukih
Sidatapa
Cempaga
Pangsusari
Rangdu
Pedawa
Asah Gobleg
Mayong
Bestala
Asah
Banyusri
G. Bratan
2098
D. Buyan
Yeh Mas
Panca Sari
D. Tamblingan
Busung Biu
Kekeran
Gunungsari
Tirta Sari
Ideran
Gobleg
Jembong
Kayuputih
Banyuatis
Munduk
Titab
Pelapuan
Bengkel
G. Tapak
1903
Kembang Merta
Candi Kuning
D. Bratan
Pura Ulun Danau Bratan
G. Lesong
1860
1877
Gesing
Kalibondan
Kedis
Uma Jero
G. Pucuk
1603
G. Nagaloka
1782
G. Pohen
2069
Bantiran
Pupuan
G. Sangkiang
2088
Batunya
G. Adeng
1615
Mayung Anyar
Tohjiwa
Gelogor
Pujungan
Sai
Pajahan
Bangsing
G. Batukaru
2276
Baturiti
Cina
Sulangai
Sandan
Batungsel
Abing
Anggsari
Soka
Tegeh
Bugbugan
Jatiluwih
Tampak Karang
Pura Luhur Batukaru
Kesambahan
Sengangan
Apuan
Tinungan
Jelantik
568
Kebonjero
Santa
Bolangan
Kembangan
Pinge

Ngis
Tembok
Bakungan
Penginyahan
Satra
Sanda
Lateng
Dausa
Sukawana
G. Penulisan
1744
Bantang
Penulisan
Catur
Belantih
Lampu
Yeh Mampeh
G.Batur
1750
Songan
Toya
Bungkah
Serai
Kintamani
Belanga
Awan
Mengsengan
Koripan
Batukaang
Batur
Pura Ulun
Danau Batur
Terunyan
Gunung Bau
Jempanang
Manikliyu
Ulian
Sekar
Mukti
Belok
D.Batur
Belancan
Kedisan
G. Abang
2152
Mengani
Penelokan
Buahan
Lambean
Banyugede
Katung
Sidan
Mangguh
Banua
Suter
Abang Batudinding
Bunutin
Sekardadi
Sekaan
Pengotan
Abuan
Langgahan
Kelod
Marga
Tengah
Kerta
Pausan
Pelak Tiying
Puregal
Singaperang
Saren
Pilan
Puakan
Pisang
Kayuambua
Tegal Suci
Keladian
Tengipis
Sritaja
Seribatu
Penyabengan
Pakusaba
Bangkled
Pura Agung
Besakih
Gambih
Penginyahan
Yang Api
Kembang
Merta
Kubakal
Besakih
Kangin
Selat Jaang
Undisan
Taro
Jasan
Pempatan
Lebih
Gunung Sari

CONTENTS

Topographic watercolor
map of Bali.

PREFACE

If you look at any civilization at any time in history, you will find people making maps.

Monastic scholars, imperialistic explorers, illiterate navigators; history is filled with cartographers. Each one of them has made maps in his or her own unique way, and each culture has formed its own unique cartographic traditions. Every civilization has devised its own method to frame the parameters of its environment and boundaries of its interests.

That is not to say that it's easy to make a map; cartography has its fair share of challenges. For example, how to create the illusion of height in a range of mountains? How to show the visual qualities of an arid plain? How to show the direction and speed of a mighty river? Essentially the question is: how to translate the 3-dimensional qualities of a place onto the flatness of a 2-dimensional surface? Throughout history, the best maps have been able to solve these visual puzzles and create maps that communicate clearly and accurately. The less successful examples are dense and illegible and remain with us only as visual oddities.

Given these challenges, why do we go to all this trouble? Are we really that afraid to get lost? Certainly, nobody wants to get mixed up in an unfamiliar place, but this is not enough to explain our obsessive map-making activity. Something else is at work here. Why do people spend hours looking over maps of places they will never visit, ruined cites of the past, or even imaginary places that never existed? Presumably, we don't worry about getting lost in an imaginary place! An answer is found by seeing map making not as a prelude to travel, but as a means of understanding our surroundings.

Maps are less about moving around in the world, and more about making sense of it. They are just the physical evidence of processes in our minds that are running all the time. We construct mental maps constantly; this is a fundamental way our minds work. This process of mental imaging is essential because we are not able to comprehend our experience of the world until we are able to imagine it and give it form. We draw lines between our separate experiences and tie them all together to form complex networks, and we map whatever is new to us; new places, new acquaintances, new cultures, new systems of belief. Over time these images in our minds develop and mature. When constructed well they can store complex patterns of information for our contemplation.

If we make these mental maps elegantly, and use their lines wisely, they can help us navigate around in our memories. But we can also make them carelessly and end up with tangled bits of strings in our imaginations, leaving us feeling lost and disoriented. This book presents a series of mapping projects completed over a 30 year period of working and living in Bali. Mapping the terrain of the island was the initial goal of these projects. But over time the focus shifted towards mapping Bali's architectural sites, its history, and the dynamics of its natural environment. Eventually its focus concentrated on mapping the lives of the Balinese people themselves, the topography of their inner lives. The book was created by stitching together the results of these various projects to produce an overall image of Bali and its people.

Before I moved to Bali, most of my learning about the world was academic. I got my knowledge about the world from classrooms and museums, and this approach has served me well. But I decided before I visited Bali to approach this new experience in a new way, not as a scholar, but as a traveller, simply keeping my eyes and ears open, making notes and sketches of this new place, writing down conversations and sketching things that were interesting. Nothing in this book is invented, all the places described and stories related in these pages were seen and heard while travelling the roads of Bali and living in its neighbourhoods. In one sense the impressions presented here can be thought of as field recordings which taken together have the potential to produce a relatively objective map of Bali at this time in history.

Whether this material has been arranged in the best possible way, whether it is relatively free from preconception and prejudice, and whether it presents a balanced view of Bali is open to debate. There will be points suggested here that will be contested by others; some things in this book will be proven wrong. Some people maintain that it is impossible to generalize about a culture, and the idea that we can "map the inner topography" of an entire culture is hopelessly naïve. Certainly the map that you eventually make of Bali will be different from this one. But these ambiguities are simply the beauty and challenges of the mapping process, and any map is best seen as the starting point for a new one to improve on.

INTRODUCTION
Mapping Balinese History

Dealing with Balinese history can be a tricky business. Very little has been written down over the ages, and those records that remain are infused with bombast and dream imagery. History has always been a convenient device of manipulation for those who want to be remembered in a good light and their enemies to be remembered as devils or fools. The historical records still available in Bali are no exception. One particular challenge is the interchangeable use of the terms "history" and "mythology". If a certain king claimed to be a direct descendant of the Gods, so it was recorded as history. Fortunately we have alternative source material we can use to unravel and augment written historical records. Here is a brief look at the methodology.

1. Our first approach is to look at the physical environment. In Bali's case this would include neighbouring islands, the seas, the winds and the prevailing currents. It would include the distance, direction and strength of the waves between the islands. Cultures are not completely dependent on their environment, but geography and surroundings have a profound influence on the development of human societies.

2. A second and more straightforward method to find out about the past is to dig in the ground and look for clues in something old. The objects discovered may

be small and humble and at first glance not very interesting. But their value is not in the aesthetics; their value is in the fact that they actually are history and can be dated with remarkable precision. Taken together, they form an aggregate of points in time that can be used as a framework for tracing the story of a culture.

3 The third method looks squarely at mythology. Mythologies have their own structure and history. Myths are not static but evolve as a series of shifting stories and images. These images can evolve from the experience of the people themselves, or they can be borrowed, or imposed by forces within or without. Taken together, these images form the points of focus that give coherence and direction to the everyday labours of society.

4 Our final method is to look at the older forms of the culture that are still present today. The point is to not to see them as "living museums"; (they do not occur in a vacuum and have undergone their own evolution and change), but they do offer a distinct vantage point to compare with the dominant forms of the culture practiced today.

PART 01

WATER AND FIRE

Many of the aboriginal Balinese, or the Bali Mula, have the same generosity of spirit that is so associated with the Balinese people generally. Other Bali Mula villages are more reserved, and some would definitely like to be left alone.

Group drawing, Sukawana, North Bali.

Bali Mula

The Bali Mula, often referred to as Bali Aga are the first Balinese, a peoples whose culture has shaped the organisation and structure of society on the island. It is tempting to say that going up on a mountain is the same as going back in time. It is not necessarily accurate but it may feel that way. Some of the villages in the more secluded foggy mountain environments appear to be the throwbacks to an earlier time. Some of them still practise a way of life that predates the form of Balinese culture more familiar today.

It is also tempting to group all these ancient villages into a single uniform social category, and this is also incorrect. Each Bali Mula village has its own way of patterning communal life. Some have strict rules about marriages within the village. Other villages forbid private possession of land: land-holding is the right of the village community.

There are, however, several things these villages have in common. They have a sophisticated ritual life that is largely supported by a strong Hindu-animist belief system. And most villages use a more egalitarian form of the Balinese language, and the Javano-Indic caste system is not found here.

Two of the most well known Bali Mula villages are Tenganan and Trunyan. Tenganan is mostly known for its astounding double ikat, a hand made cloth which is extremely difficult to create. It also has a ceremony where the young men hit each other in mock battle with pandanus leaves. These leaves have sharp thorns along the edge and these skirmishes always draw blood. This is necessary because this is a human blood sacrifice, an important ritual to ensure the wellbeing of the village.

Trunyan also has a particularly notorious ritual that draws visitors to its shores on the edge of Lake Batur. After a villager dies and undergoes the essential rituals, the body is placed on the ground in the cemetery area and left there to decompose.

The Bali Mula do not see their life as an exercise in looking backward. Rather they see their particular cultural beliefs as a form of exclusivity, something to be proud of.

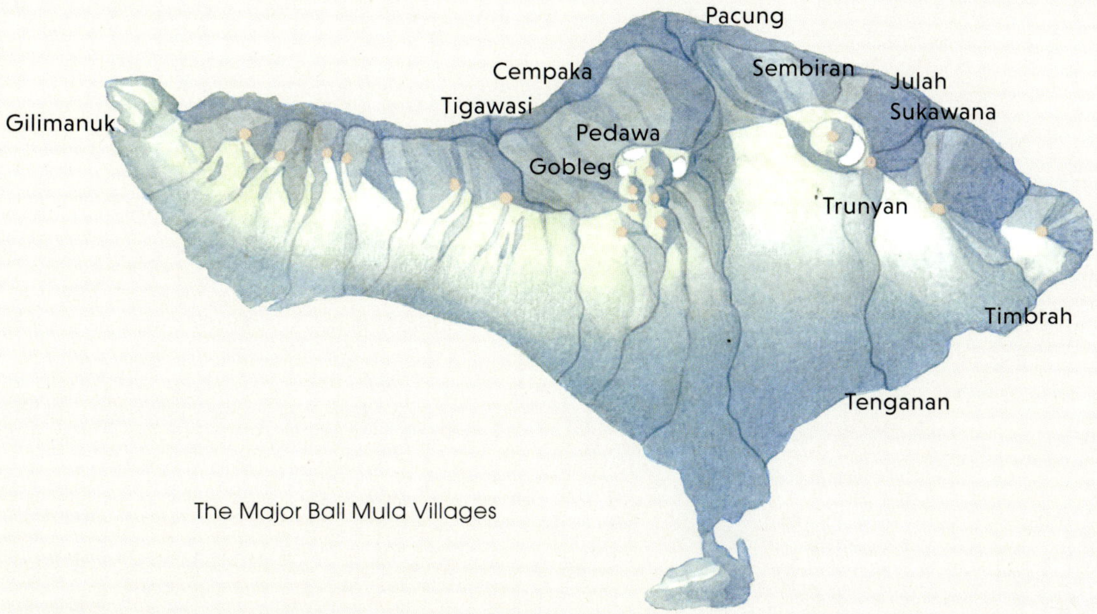

The Major Bali Mula Villages

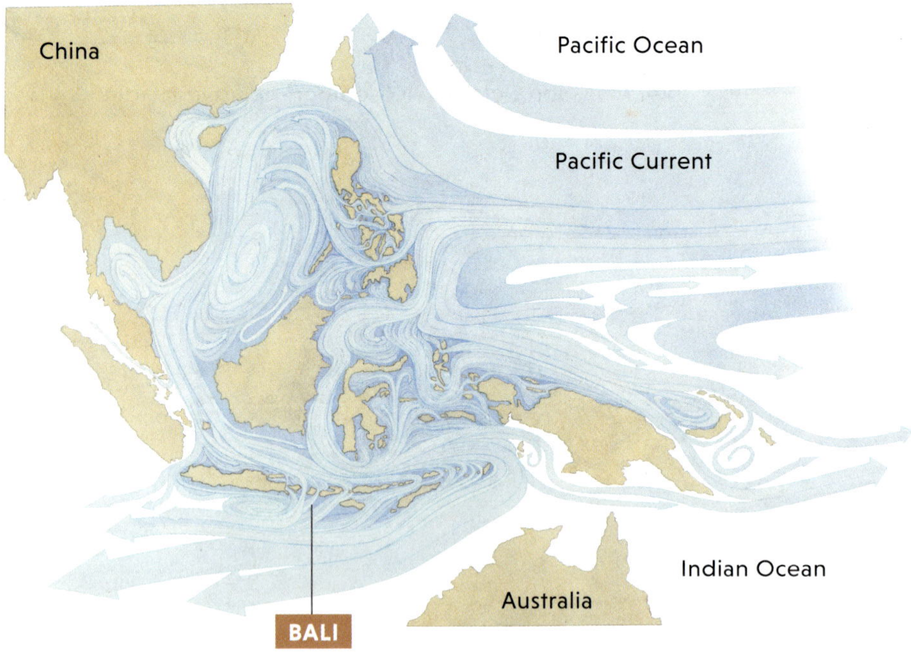

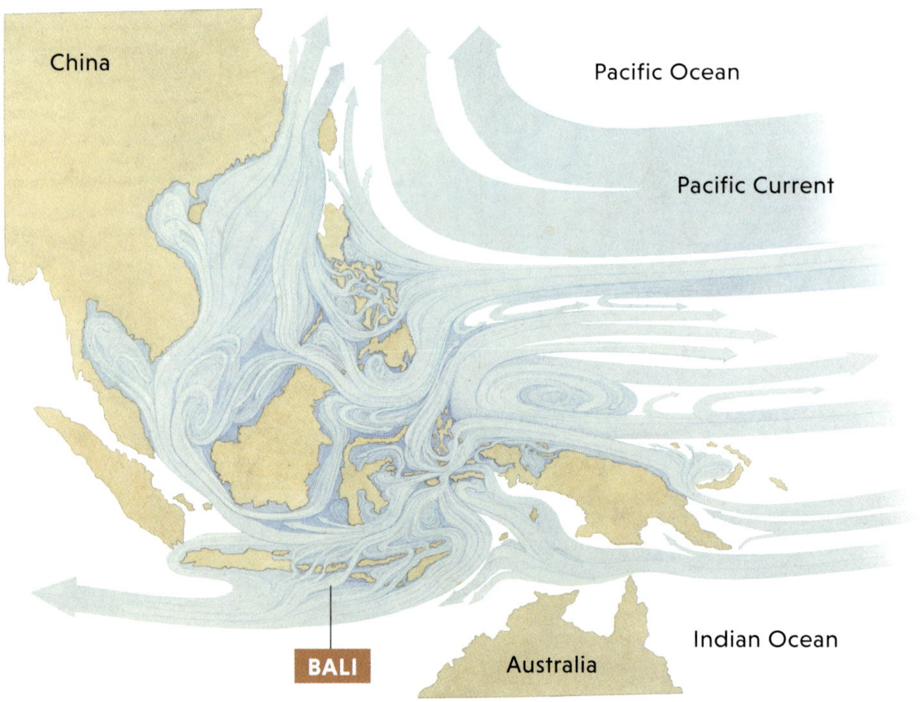

Current and Winds

Bali is one island in the midst of 17,000 other islands in the Indonesian Archipelago. The area enclosed by this group of islands is roughly the size of Europe. Needless to say there is a lot of water here.

Just as the restless rumbling of the earth's interior just below the earth's surfaces has shaped Indonesia's geography, the dynamics above and below the surface of the oceans have also had a deep impact on the patterns of island life.

There are great currents in the world's oceans. In the Pacific ocean, for example, huge amounts of water flow from east to west in the aptly named Pacific Current. These currents bombard the easternmost islands of Indonesia and bring countless tons of sea life into the interior of the Archipelago. This mighty current is broken up into complex patterns of smaller currents and eddies as it careens through the many islands in the interior of the Archipelago. There are detailed charts used by navigators to help them find a way through these currents as they shift and even change direction during the seasonal changes. In earlier days of ocean navigation the vessels were small and so the waves and currents were a significant factor in their voyages. The maps made by these early sailors were composed of bamboo strips and shells representing waves and islands, the only details these sailors needed to know.

The winds were easier to understand. Broadly speaking, for six months they blew in one direction and then they shifted and blew the other way, year after year for as long as the earth has been in the form we recognize. Presumably, it didn't take long for the ancient sailors to figure out that they had six months to travel in one direction, and six months to return home again. Eventually, firmly established trading routes were set up between India and China. Indonesia is located about halfway between these two giants and became a pivotal port of call for ships sailing between them.

Bali is located at the farthest point south in this network of trade. When the first visitors anchored on the northern coast of Bali to trade they found an island populated with a people who were a mix of two racial types. These were either the prehistoric migrants who passed by Bali between 17,000 and 50,000 years ago on their way to New Guinea and Australia. These people are characterized by dark skin and curly hair. Or they could have been descendants of peoples who travelled south from the Asian mainland about 3000 years ago on far-reaching voyages, the farthest of which ended up across the Indian Ocean at the islands of Madagascar. These people are known for their light skin and straight black hair. The intermingling of the two people formed the basic physical characteristics and linguistic foundation that are still evident in Balinese society today.

The early culture was enriched by ideas and spiritual beliefs that followed in the wake of the early traders, especially the Hindu and Buddhist beliefs from India. Importantly, these ideas were adopted freely by the early Balinese, there is no evidence of colonizing or coercion in this gradual absorption.

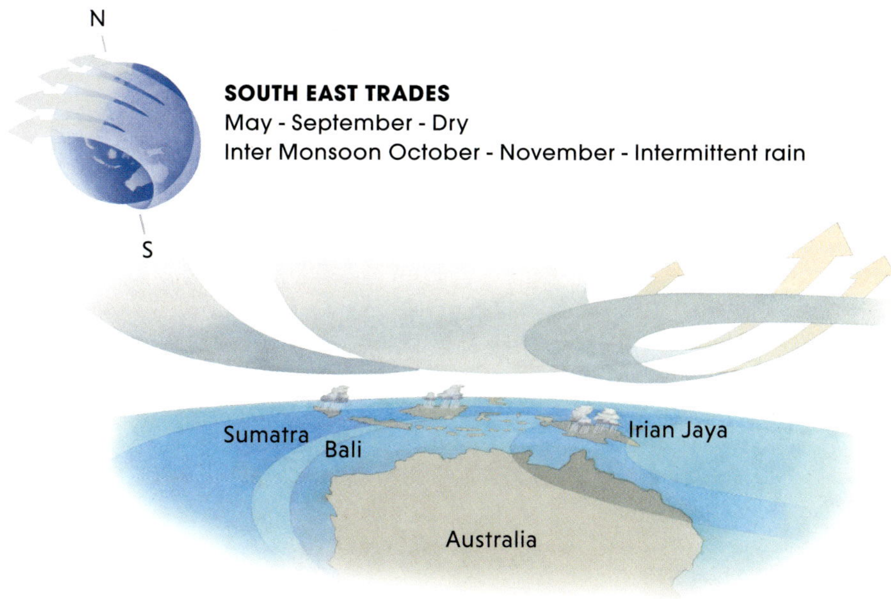

These winds blow over the Australian Continent to the north west and don't pick up much moisture.

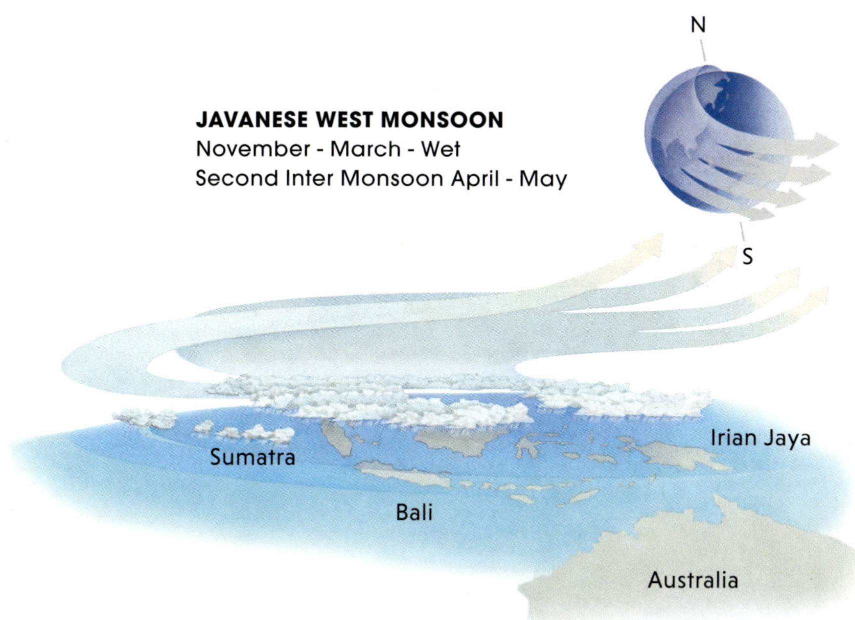

The winds begin from the East Asian Mainland and blow to the south east over the pacific Ocean picking up ample moisture. These long rows of clouds provide daily rains to the Indonesian Archipelago.

Development of Wet Rice Cultivation

Uncultivated site with single river.

Early lowland cultivated site using water from a single river.

Fully cultivated site.

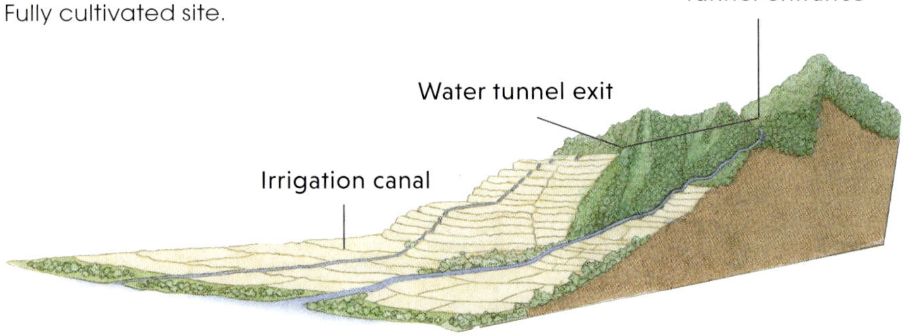

Hydrology & Water Societies

The earliest settlers on the island were in a passive role as they tried to make a living. They either hunted or planted whatever they could in the land around them. As these settlements became more established, the people started to manipulate the environment to suit their needs. The topography of Bali is well suited as a water delivery system, and this is an essential element in the implementation of wet rice cultivation. Early attempts to direct irrigation water were along rivers and swamps, or at water springs on hillsides. Eventually, individual mountain ridges became irrigated by long water tunnels starting upstream on major rivers. These developed as separate irrigation systems. The importance of these tunnels and the men who built them is underscored by the fact that one of the earliest known Balinese inscriptions mentions the dealings between one group of tunnel builders and a local king.

An important aspect of these irrigated 'water mountains' (Lansing) is that they seem to be individually governed. They did not require an all-powerful king with centralized power to manage the entire irrigation system. Since the beginning, these agricultural communities seem to have been self-governed by collective labour. They were pre-caste and this type of social organization is still reflected in some aspects of Bali Mula villages.

Nevertheless water societies were not independent of each other; wet rice cultivation requires a high degree of cooperation. As these communities began to develop and expand there needed to be an uphill-downhill cooperation in matters relating to water regulation and pest control. Eventually this extended beyond individual ridges, incorporating different water mountains running east to west. So although there remained a considerable amount of autonomy between different water societies, they became increasingly interrelated and interdependent. The inter-village level social group that oversees all these activities is known as *Subak*.

The Goddess of the Lake

Eventually there needed to be a single point of focus so that the entire social enterprise didn't spin into chaos. The image chosen to provide this focus was the image of a mandala placed squarely in one of the mountain lake, Lake Batur. This image was intended as the spiritual abode of the Goddess of the Lake. The human connection to the Goddess and her Mandala was the head priest of the mountain temple, Ulun Danu. This priest served as her human consort. This priest is chosen from the family clan called the Black Wood Clan (Dadia Kayu Silam), one of the oldest clans on the island. He is responsible for all the water societies in Bali, settling disputes over water supply and ritual requirements; he also helps with various logistic matters. It could be said that this priest provides the point of focus for the entire operation, and gives meaning to the labour in the fields.

Temple Ulun Danu, Batur Lake, Central Bali.

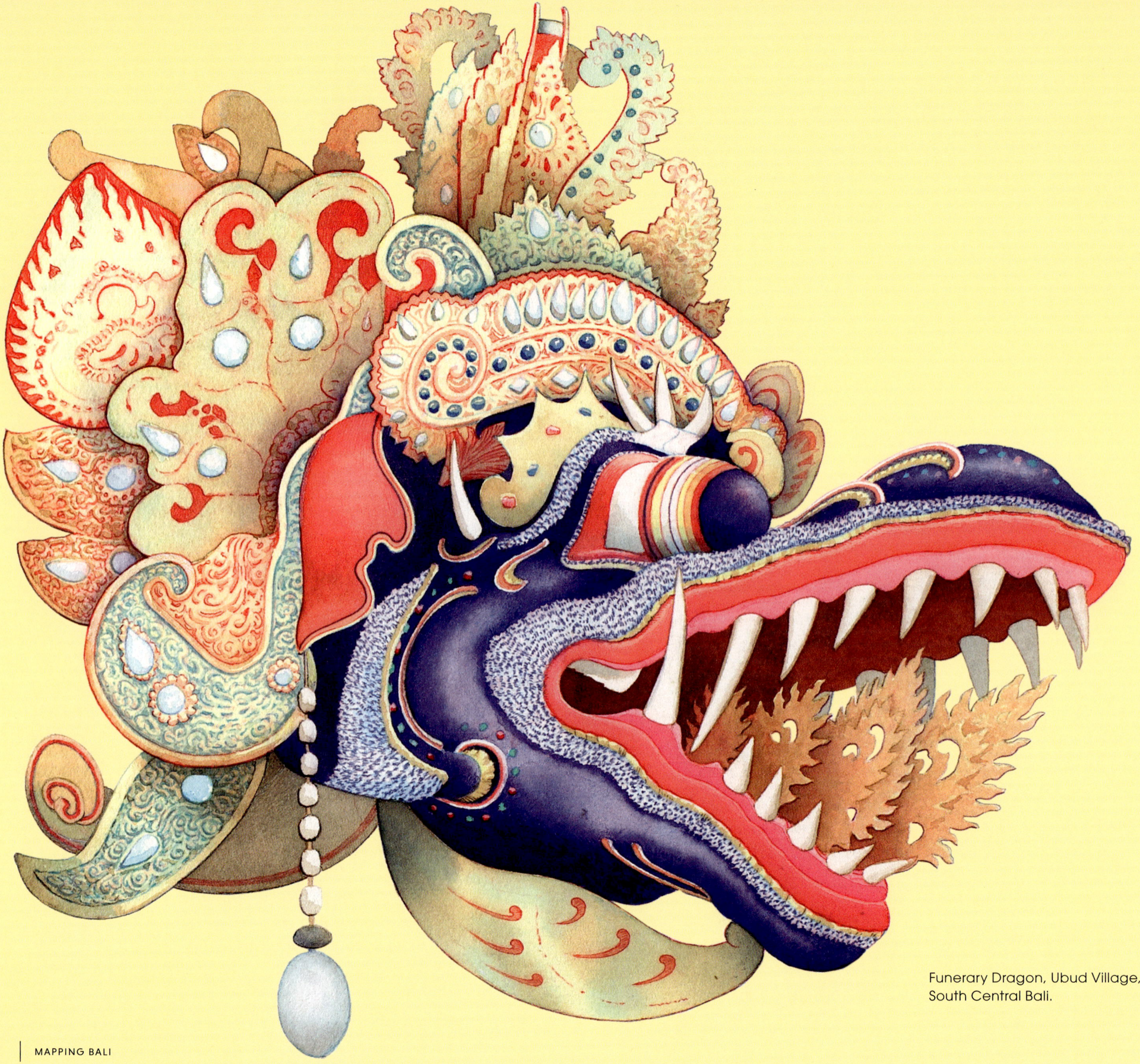

Funerary Dragon, Ubud Village,
South Central Bali.

Holograms of God

Relative sizes, Bali and Java

The fledgling *Subak* irrigation scheme was firmly in place by the end of the first millennium. About this time Bali became increasingly under the shadow of its big neighbour to the west, Java. The earliest relations between Java and Bali were mutually beneficial and peaceful. Relationships between the various kingdoms were accomplished by intermarriage between the Javanese and Balinese royal houses. This interaction reached a degree of formality in 984 when an edict was proclaimed that Javanese would become the official language of Bali. From that point on Bali became increasingly under Javanese control and relations increasingly militaristic. The first military campaign against Bali was in 1282, and a second promulgated by the mighty Majapahit Dynasty in 1343.

This influence on Balinese life from Javanese dominance proved to be an important element in the shaping of the modern Balinese culture. Unlike earlier influences that seeped into the consciousness of the local population over an extended period of time, these new images of culture were imposed by political decree, in the form of a colonizing myth. The indigenous Balinese were told that their culture was coarse and ill-formed. They were told that a superior culture was being brought to them by their Javanese conquerors. This colonizing myth supplied an image of a new way of life to the Balinese that would be acceptable to them, and was needed to justify the presence of the new rulers.

The central tenet of this myth was the image of the king himself. The king was a spiritual figurehead, the manifestation of Siwa, a hologram of God. Like a royal mirror, the king's image reflected spiritual perfection to the ruling nobility, then reflected further down to the local population (Geertz). This image of the God King found its earthly seat in the temple of Besakih on the foothills of Mount Agung, an active volcano where the king identified himself with the God of fire. The colonizing myth of the Majapahit goes as far as to claim that the new rulers actually brought Mount Agung with them to Bali, such was their might, and their attention to detail!

The greatest of these kings did their jobs well and provided an additional point of focus and coherence to the population at large. They brought a greater degree of richness and sophistication in the arts than had been known in Bali. But mirrors are prone to get dusty and not reflect very well. The weaker of these kings were less like holograms of God and more like imitators of Elvis, prancing about their palaces in opiated silliness. Political models that rely on this type of image require a finely tuned sense of political theatre and not every king was up to the challenge. Ultimately, however the whole enterprise was successful enough. The new leaders proclaimed themselves to be the new insiders, and the indigenous Balinese the new outsiders on the island of their birth. The Balinese even lost the collective memory of an earlier culture and who they had once been.

Gunung Kawi, Tampak Siring
Village, Central Bali.

Fusing Fire and Water

It is the relationship and competition between two images - the Lake Goddess with her Mandala of agricultural, egalitarian power and the God King with his caste hierarchy - that have formed the landscape of the Balinese soul. Both of these images can be actively seen throughout the daily life of Bali today. The water image is most clearly seen in the *Subak* organisation and the fire image in the networks of clan temples in Bali. Sometimes these two images coexist in everyday life with people bouncing back and forth between them. At other times they are in conflict and create social tension. At notable times they are held in balance and synthesize into an entirely new image. This doesn't happen very often—the fusing of fire and water is not an easy matter, but the result is powerful when it does happen.

The wisest Balinese rulers have tried to produce this kind of fusion. They have worked together with the older agricultural orders to provide a measure of stability so the farmers could go about their work. They worked with two venerable family clans, the Pasek and Bandesa, to work as intermediaries between the rulers and the villages. These relationships are still functioning today.

A physical reminder of the dynamics between kings and villages is the area between the Petanu and Pakerisan Rivers. These rivers begin high in the mountainous area around Lake Batur where an important temple was built (and is still located), Pura Penulisan. The rivers flow southward (*kelod*) towards the ocean, passing through the present day village of Pejeng. Around the environs of Pejeng are located many of Bali's oldest and most venerated temples; the present day Archeological Museum is located in this area. The ancient temples located along these two rivers, from *kaja* to *kelod* (or the mountains to the sea) are like a string of pearls out lining the activities of the Balinese kings throughout history.

Major Archaeology Sites

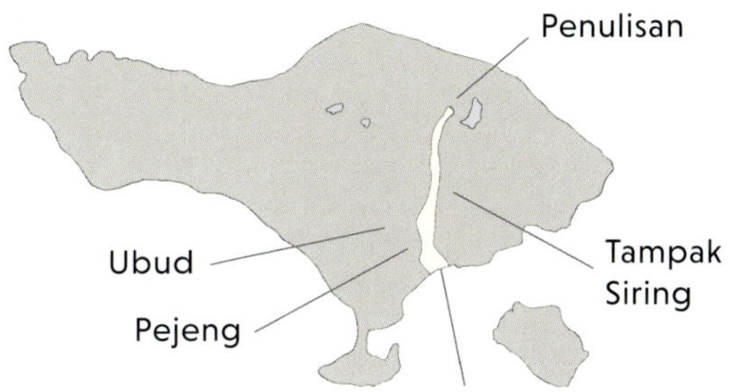

The land between the Petanu and Pakerisan rivers

Gunung Kawi is one of the most interesting sites located in this area. Dating from the 8th Century, it is accessible by walking down a steep river bank surrounded by rice fields. There is not complete agreement as to the purpose of this site, but the best evidence suggests that this is the site of funerary monuments for one of Bali's most respected kings, Anak Wungsu. Located within this area is a series of meditation chambers cut into the rock of the hillside. Their walls are massive and silent, except for the trickles of ground water flowing from them.

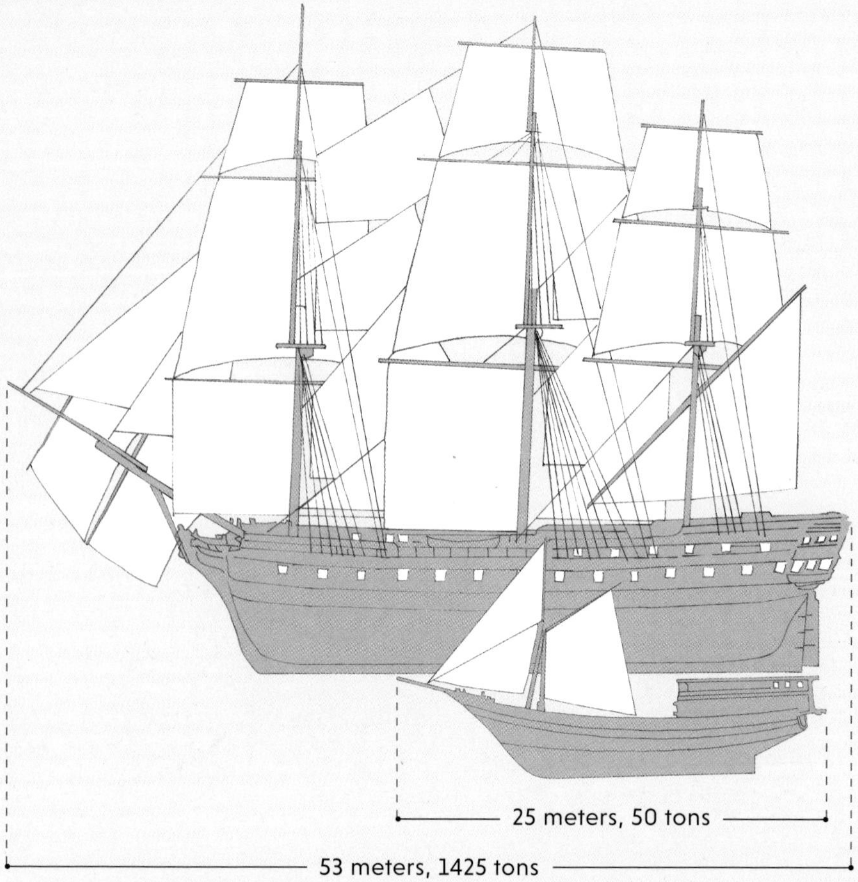

A comparative illustration showing two different types of sailing craft seen in the Indonesian Archipelago between the 17th and 19th centuries. The first is a traditional Indonesian sailing ship, a Phenisi, and the second a typical European armed cargo ship commonly called an East Indiaman. This illustration shows the comparative might of the colonial fleet, from the shape of the hull to the rows of cannons along the side. This armament made it clear that the colonial powers meant business.

Breaking the Spell

Perhaps it is only possible to maintain this intricate balance of cultural images in a small, self-contained, and inward-looking place like Bali. Too much attention from the outside world would threaten the entire endeavour—like turning up the lights in a theatre while the show was still going on.

Even though Bali has had international contacts since the days of the earliest traders, these contacts did not substantially affect the rhythms of everyday Balinese life. The kings did set up trading relationships with various foreigners throughout history, but the management of these concerns was taken care of by their trading agents. They oversaw the details of the business and simply gave a commission to the king. This allowed the kings to be mercantile without having to do the numbers.

All this began to change when the colonial European powers began to arrive to Bali in increasing numbers in the 17th Century. As naval architecture in Europe became more sophisticated, these ships took longer and longer voyages and brought back larger cargos. They came for trade, and if they found anything worth trading they returned with military might to control this trade. First came the Portuguese, then the Dutch, the English (for a short time) and the Dutch again. In 1908 the Dutch finally were able to control the entire island of Bali after a long military campaign, and they quickly began to rearrange the way Balinese life was organized. Among other things they decided to codify and systemize the fluid relationship of power between the kings and the agricultural communities. It seemed self-evident and perhaps more equitable to the Dutch to replace this complex and sometimes chaotic balance of power with a more concrete political reality. In the words of Clifford Geertz, "the poetics of power were replaced with the mechanics of power".

But in the end, this tampering with the culture proved devastating. It eliminated the need for a king to be an image of power, one of the central images that gave meaning to daily life at that time. It is dangerous to disrupt the fundamental images a culture uses to orient itself. The loss of this cultural coherence by the simple act of straightening up and smoothing out Bali's fluidity is widely blamed for setting into motion a series of power struggles on Bali. Competition between various groups eventually reached a point of crisis that resulted in a meltdown of Balinese society in the 1965 Indonesian political struggles. The anarchy and frenzied chaos resulted in the deaths of so many people that is rare to find a Balinese person who will talk about it. As the witnesses to this tragedy eventually die, these events will be transformed into one more mythological chapter in Bali's long dream of history.

PART 02

ROCKS AND WATER

First Glimpses

Bali has long been identified with its beautiful terraced rice fields, and rightly so, they are magnificent. But the history of their construction and the management of the water that passes through them is less well-known.

Until the modern era, this is what Bali's southern coast looked like. It is an enticing image of a fertile place that may have lured some sailors in for a closer view, and perhaps a premature death. A prudent sailor would have stayed a healthy distance away to avoid being caught in the strong currents and dangerous reefs that ring the southern coast.

But the earliest visitors were probably not sailors at all; they were more likely to have been wandering groups of people from the Asian mainland, hopping down between these islands as early as 50,000 years ago. The first sailors arrived much later, about 3,000 years ago. These were the legendary Austronesian seafarers who covered an amazingly large area of the Pacific Ocean in their explorations.

There may have been some true explorers among Bali's first visitors, people with a curiosity for all things that lie over the horizon. But these people were rare. Most explorers who would have visited Bali were traders. Commerce was the major motivation to undertake these dangerous and uncertain journeys. Eventually, other interested parties tagged along with the merchants, introducing new political systems and spiritual beliefs from around the world to these isolated places.

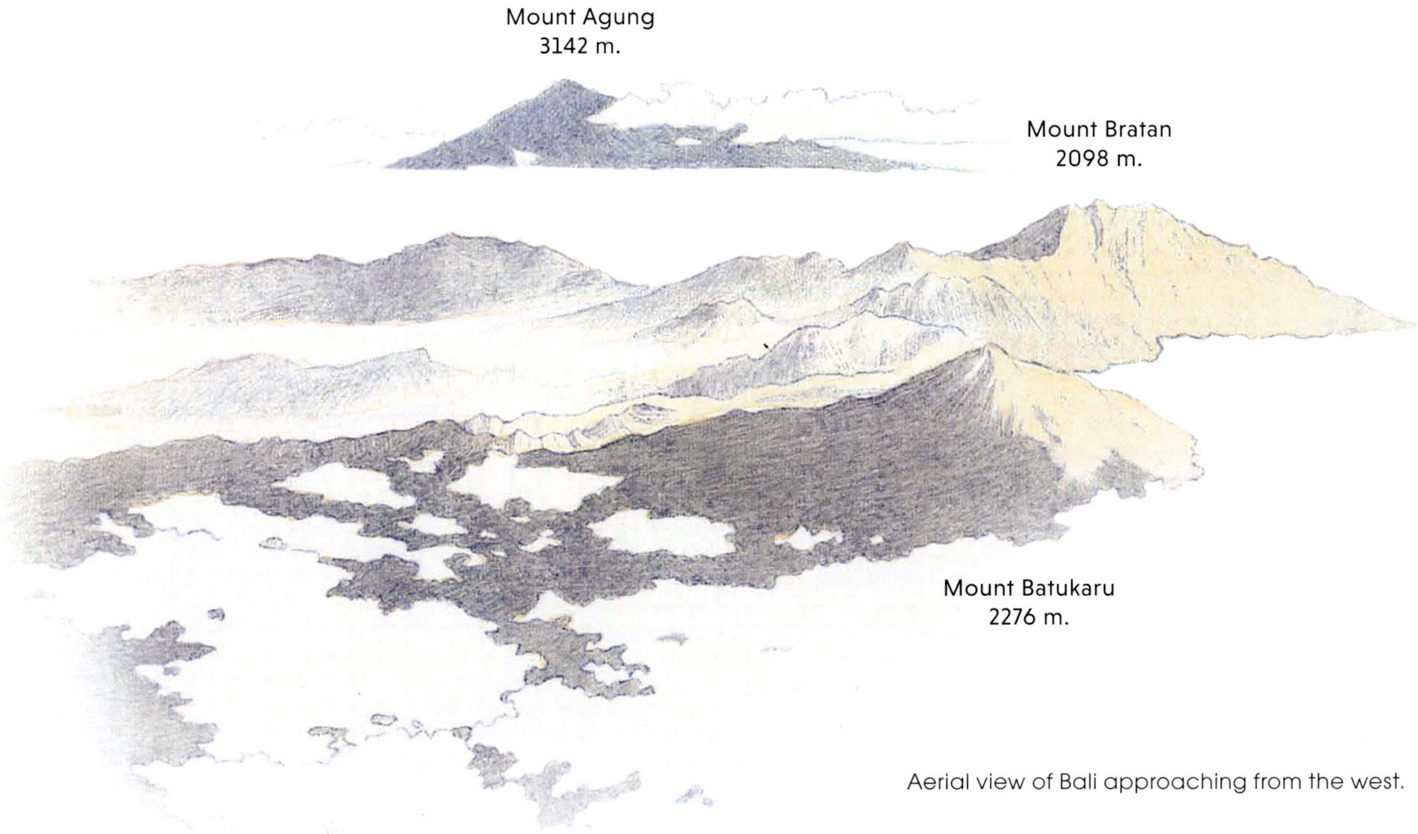

Aerial view of Bali approaching from the west.

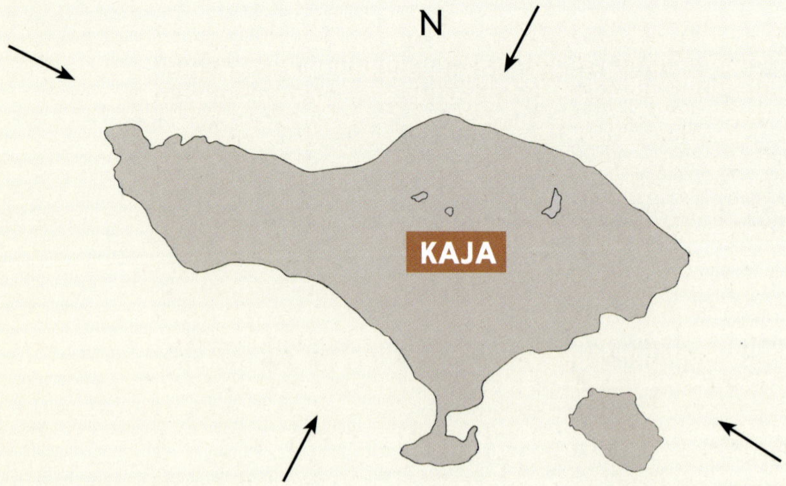

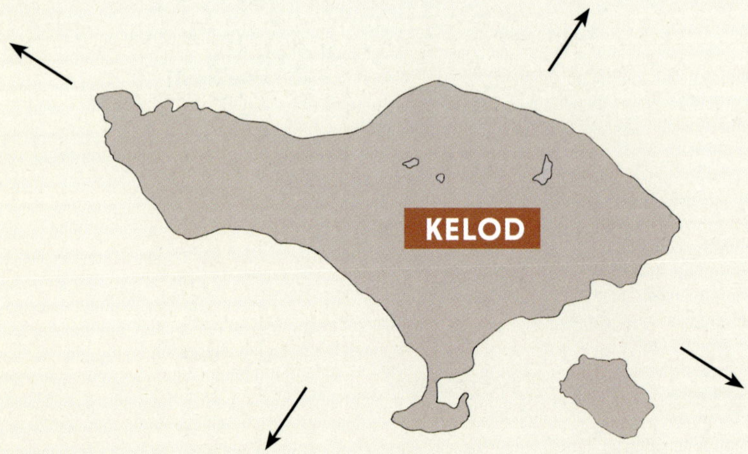

Kaja and Kelod

The mountains are Bali's predominant point of focus, sometimes hidden from sight, but rarely forgotten. They provide one pole in a two-pole system of orientation that is central to Balinese thought and action. According to Balinese thinking, you are either moving toward the mountains or away from them (to the sea). It sounds simple enough but it is loaded with meaning, as we will see in the following pages.

It is important to realise from the start that *kaja-kelod* is not simply a directional relationship: it is a system of orientation. The two opposing directions of *kaja-kelod* change direction depending where you are on the island. For a person in south Bali, *kaja* is to the north, to someone on the north coast it is to the south. The central mountains remain the point of focus wherever you might be. This often causes confusion for a person born in the south moving to the north: he or she has to flip his or her direction for *kaja-kelod*, and this causes much confusion and misunderstanding.

There is a clear preference for *kaja* over *kelod*. *Kaja* is associated with the mountains, symbols of clarity and holiness. Conversely, *kelod* is associated with the ocean, the realm of confusion and dissolution. But this doesn't mean that the Balinese flock to the mountains and shun the sea. *Kaja-kelod* has less to do with geography and more with how the Balinese see themselves. To face *kaja* is to look into the island, the village and family clan, towards all that is stable and knowable. To face *kelod*, on the other hand, is to look squarely at things unknown, to outside places and people, to face uncertainty and disorientation. Balinese culture discourages any view outside itself, it actively absorbs its members into the group as a whole. It is not surprising that *kelod* is seen as an unfavorable direction and way of life.

View of Mount Agung from the South, Central Bali.

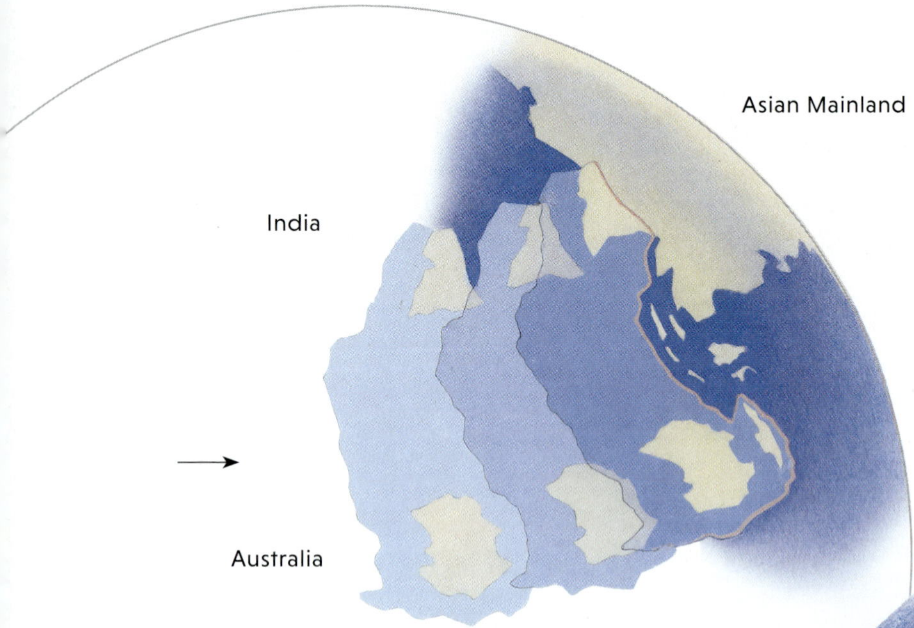
Asian Mainland
India
Australia

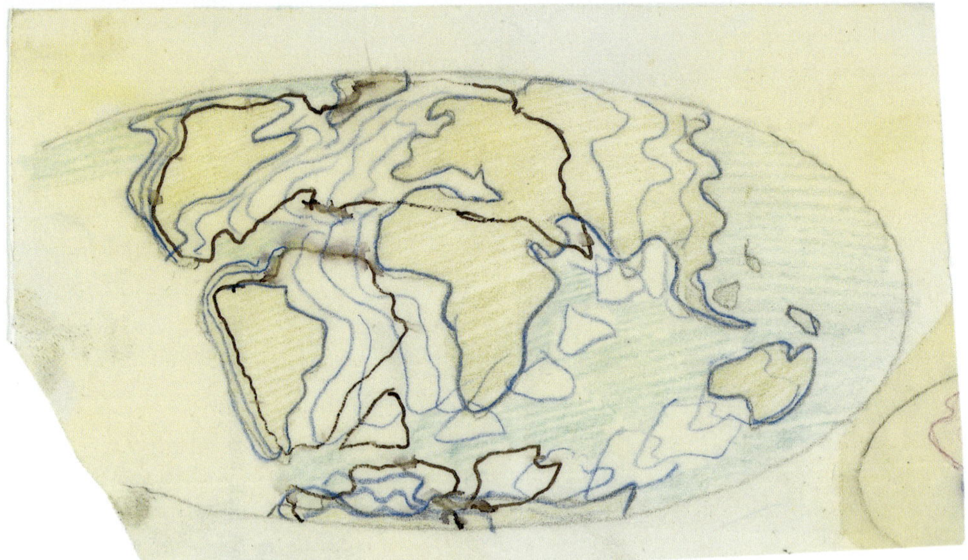

Himalaya Range
Asian Mainland
India
Ring of Fire
Pacific Ocean
Indian Ocean
BALI
Australia

Rocks

There is a less abstract way that these mountains can help understanding life on Bali. If we stripped them of all their symbolic associations, the mountains remain as huge piles of volcanic rock, powerful evidence of how Bali was formed many millennia ago.

Bali is located in one of the most dynamic and complex regions of volcanic activity on the planet; even geologists themselves cannot completely agree on mapping its dynamics. But a simple geological model can be reliably used toward a basic understanding of how Bali island originated. This model is based on two main dynamics.

The first dynamic depicts the earth as a huge magnet, creating a large magnetic field around and within the planet.

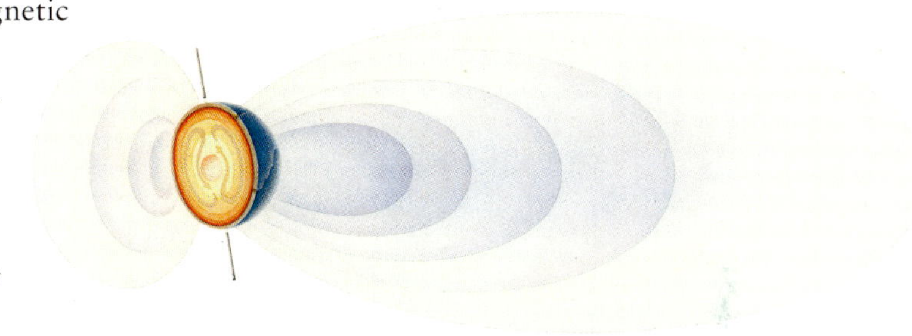

The second dynamic characterises the earth as made up of layers of semi-molten rock, with only the immediate crust having cooled and solidified.

Geological tension is caused by the interaction between these two dynamics; the magnetic forces acting upon the molten, unstable layers beneath the thin crust, causing these layers to shift and flow. Occasionally this movement causes the brittle outer layer to crack.

The resulting broken pieces of the outer crust are called plates. The thicker of them form the great continents, the thinner ones form the ocean's floor. The restless interior of the earth continuously pushes and pulls these plates and causes them to drift and collide with each other.

One of these continental plates is called the Indo-Australian plate. It has been relatively active during earth's long history and has moved eastward from earth's initial unified land mass until it collided with the Asian mainland, the Euro-Asian plate, hundreds of millions of years ago. One of the results of this collision was the fusing of the Indian subcontinent with the rest of Asia. The 'rubble' caused by this line of collision is commonly known as the Himalayan mountain range. The other result was the collision between the eastern edge of the Indo-Australian plate into the western edge of the Eurasian plate. The rubble from this collision did not rise above the surface as a great mountain range, but was forced back into the molten interior of the earth.

None of these movements happened quickly; these movements are so slow that we can't perceive them. But there is so much material involved and the forces so great that this line of collision, from Sumatera to Irian Jaya, is one of the most critical areas of geological stress on the planet. The cracks in these two plates caused by their collision allows molten material to be released to the surface, forming volcanoes. The series of volcanoes along this line of collision is famously called 'the ring of fire' and this beautifully describes them. The eruption and re-eruption of these volcanoes formed the string of islands along this line, including Bali.

Each news report from Indonesia about a volcano, tsunami or earthquake is a powerful reminder of the continued movement of the Indo-Australian plate into the Asian mainland. The earth is never static but is constantly forming itself. If you are reading this in Bali you can be sure that there are massive forces quietly at work beneath your feet.

Underwater topographic map of the islands in the environs of Bali.

Halmahera
Irian Jaya
Sulawesi
Seram
Buru
Aru
Wetar
Alor
Sumbawa
Flores
Sumba

Water

The surface of the great oceans is evaporated by the sun, forms into clouds, and eventually is released back to the surface as rain. Bali gets its fair share of rain, at least for part of the year. During the dry season (usually April to October) there is very little if any rain. During those months, winds blow from the southeast over the Australian continent and don't pick up enough moisture to form substantial rain clouds. But during the rest of the year the opposite is true. The winds switch direction and blow from the northwest over the vast Pacific Ocean forming long lines of heavy, moisture-laden clouds. When these reach Bali there are almost daily rains, and this channels the rhythm of daily life. The constant situation of being wet or recently wet creates its own challenges and fosters a kind of group spirit among the local population.

Mount Agung Seen From The West, Central Bali.

"The morning commute, on a motorcycle, in rush hour traffic, during a flash rain storm. Trying to keep work clothes or school uniforms dry and presentable while only being protected by a thin plastic poncho. Sometimes the challenge is too much. Look for a large tree or overhanging roof and join the others waiting out the storm. Sometimes a roof doesn't provide the hoped-for shelter; after all it is constructed only of clay tiles over a wooden framework. The rain water leaks between the gaps in these tiles and runs down the cement walls, making it even more difficult for the paint trying to adhere to this incompatible surface. The water also drips into aluminum pots or plastic buckets arranged on the floor. The different rhythms and intensities of sound created by this dripping water, all night long, can be thought of as an extended performance of minimalist music (but only if you are in a very good mood and don't mind a little insomnia)."

Mountain Lakes

After the storm some of the rainwater runs back to the ocean, some of it evaporates away, some of it is stored as ground water, and some of it is held in Bali's four caldera-type mountain lakes.

Here is the geological process by which a volcano becomes a caldera lake.

1. The initial volcano is formed, and the lava chimney is plugged up by hardened lava.
2. Molten lava from earth's interior continues to push up on the plugged chimney until the pressure cannot be contained, and the peak eventually explodes.
3. The crater caused by this explosion eventually fills with rain water to form a lake. Sometimes a new volcano forms from the same lava chimney and rises out from the lake.

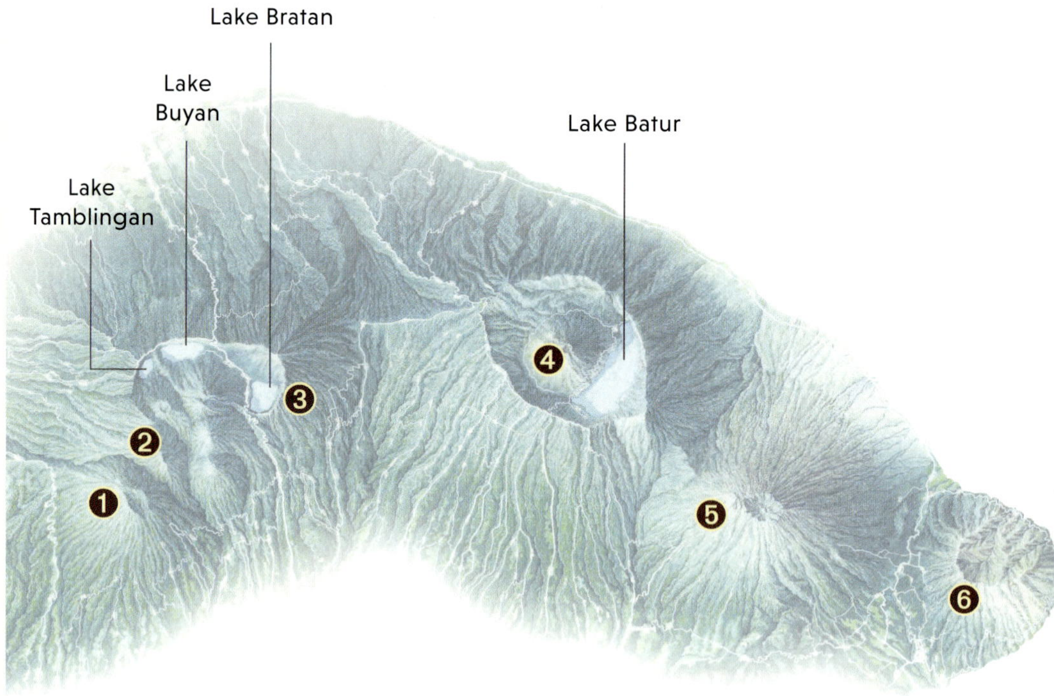

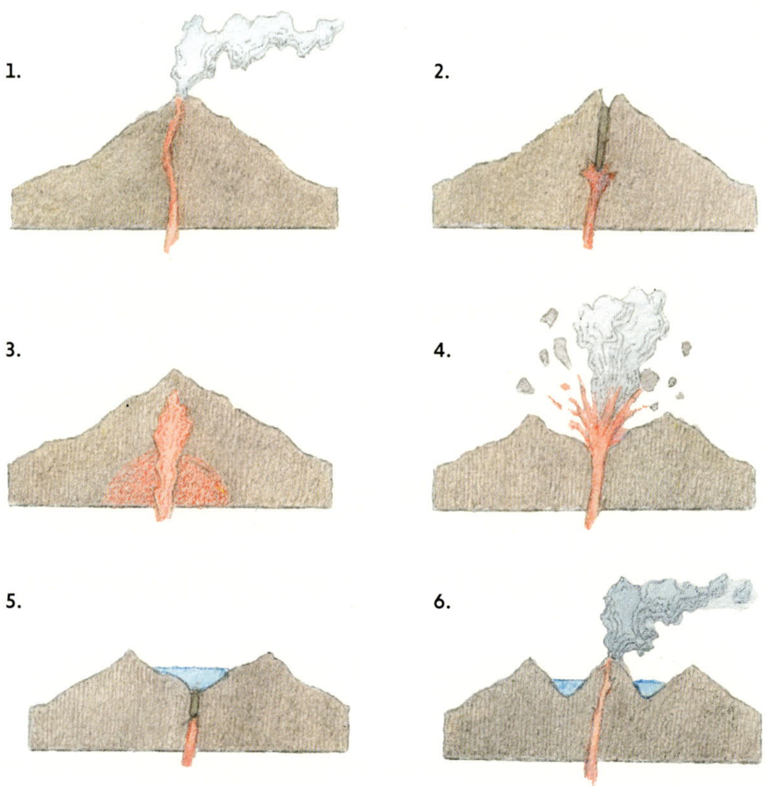

Looking at Bali's topography along a line running from west to east it becomes evident that several of Bali's volcanoes have had multiple eruptions. Starting from the west: Mount Batu Karu ❶ seems to have exploded its summit at some point in its history. Mount Lesong ❷ has apparently done the same thing. Mount Bratan ❸ shows a series of additional volcanoes located immediately to the south, splintering the original caldera into three lakes: Tamblingan, Buyan, and Bratan. Mount Batur ❹ has the most intact and nearly symmetrical caldera with a lake of the same name. It also is the most active volcano in Bali at this time. Mount Agung ❺ lost its summit in a massive explosion in 1963. This cataclysm caused extensive damage to the island and some areas In the north east have yet to recover. Mount Seraya ❻ would have become a caldera if it had not lost its northern rim. If this caldera had remained intact it would probably have become Bali's fifth lake, Danau Seraya.

These lakes with their contrasting images of fire and water are the source of many myths. They are magnificent at any time of day and in any type of weather. This is a view of Lake Tamblingan, on the northern rim looking south.

Statue and water spring,
Telaga Waja, Central Bali.

Rock Springs

All this water doesn't just sit in these lakes—the mountains themselves are full of cracks and fissures. The water leaks out, making its way through the bedrock by means of subterranean passages. Eventually the water re-emerges from the ground forming rock springs. The water bubbling out from the sides of rocky hills is cool, clean, and delicious, especially after a hard day of work in the sun. It is not surprising that the Balinese regard many of these springs to be sacred. The water from a selected few of them is considered to have powerful spiritual properties.

Bathing pool, Goa Gajah temple complex, South Bali.

Tirta Empul temple complex, Tampak Siring, Central Bali.

One of the sources of the Ayung River near the village of Nungnung, Central Bali.

Rivers

Some of the rainwater takes a different route. It is neither stored in the mountain lakes, nor absorbed into the soil, but directed by the island's topography to form rivers and streams. These begin modestly, high in the mountains, but eventually build in strength as they reach the lowlands. Over millennia, these rivers have carved deep valleys into the hillsides, almost as if there were fingers coming down the mountains to the sea. It is easier to travel north and south along the ridges of these finger-like hills than to travel east to west. The earliest inhabitants adapted to this topography and built foot paths that followed these ridges instead of challenging them. Eventually, a network of roads has been built that follows these earlier foot paths. The majority of these present day roads go up and down the hills; only a few cross between them.

The rivers on the north side are largely seasonal as this is the arid side of the island. Many of these rivers flow only after a strong rain, with the deep thundering sound (more felt than heard) of large boulders swept up in the current. On the south side of the island, most rivers flow year round, first rushing down the hillsides and then meandering through the gentle alluvial plain. Twisting through the thick vegetation, the rivers form quiet grottoes, shaded areas perfect for taking a bath.

Bathing Spot, Blah Kiuh Village, Central Bali.

One of the greatest pleasures of tropical life is an afternoon bath with family or friends in a cool river. Balinese people used to bathe quite openly but got tired of being stared at by outsiders, so they now concentrate this pastime in more secluded places. Women and men each have their own places to bathe. These locations are separated just far enough for some privacy, but they are also located just close enough for the younger or more active members of either gender to slyly tease and catch glimpses of each other. Small families or groups of friends often bathe together, exchanging the local gossip and enjoying the spectacle of the afternoon sky turning into evening."

A series of irrigation canals and dams,
Dalung village, South Bali.

Directed Water

What a shame to have all this water pass by and not to put it to work! The topography of the island is already well suited as a water management system. With the mountain lakes and ground water as the source, and the rivers as the delivery system, an irrigation system is already half finished. To complete the task, countless generations of farmers have carved into the hills and plains to add to what nature had started. The end result is a massive water management system complete with tunnels through the hills, aqueducts, dams, canals, and finally the rice terraces themselves. It's like an island with its plumbing exposed. Taken as a whole it is a beautifully articulated sculpture in the earth which could stand alone as a work of art.

But this is just the beginning: this system is just the framework for something even more intricate. The water enters at the highest point and is directed and carefully coordinated to slowly flow through the different pathways to irrigate specific fields at specific times. Sometimes a field needs to be wet, at other times it needs to be dry. The different requirements of the rice plants at the various stages of their growth need to be carefully monitored. If this is not done, the rice plants will fail due to lack of water, or be destroyed by pests and disease because of too much water.

An aquaduct just north of Tampak Siring Village, Central Bali.

Sayan
Kedewatan
Penestanan
Sebali
Bentuyung
Ubud
Petulu
Gentong
Melayang
Teges
Peliatan
Laplapan
Tengkulak
Titiapi
Sala
Pejeng Kelod
Pejeng
Bedulu

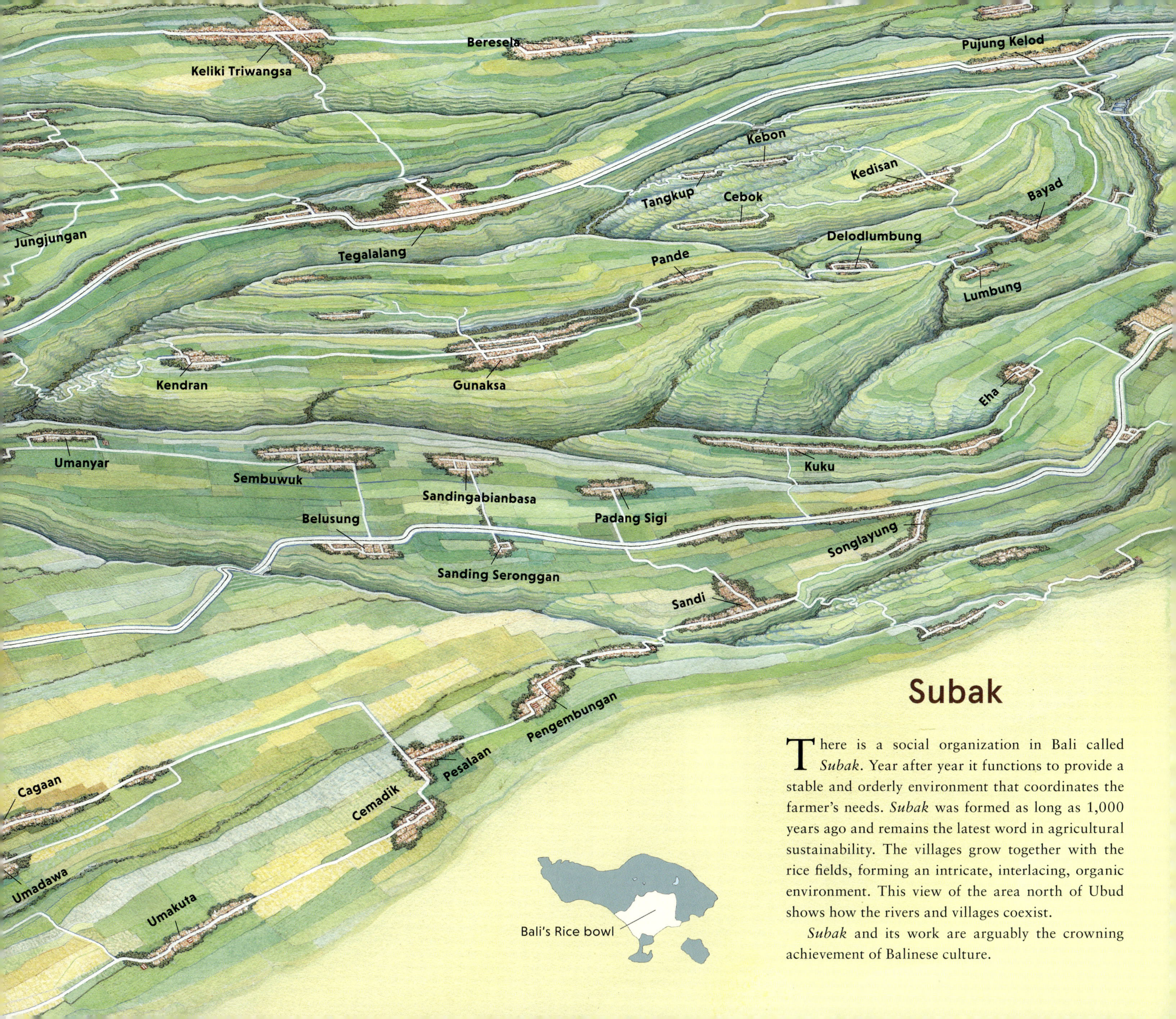

Subak

There is a social organization in Bali called *Subak*. Year after year it functions to provide a stable and orderly environment that coordinates the farmer's needs. *Subak* was formed as long as 1,000 years ago and remains the latest word in agricultural sustainability. The villages grow together with the rice fields, forming an intricate, interlacing, organic environment. This view of the area north of Ubud shows how the rivers and villages coexist.

Subak and its work are arguably the crowning achievement of Balinese culture.

Field drawings on a windy day, South Central Bali.

The Rice Fields

The unwanted guests are the birds that feast on the ripe grains of rice. All sorts of noisemaking devices have been fabricated to scare them away. These contraptions usually have a propeller that klacks tin against tin all night and day (as long as the wind holds out). Sometimes this noise is not frightening enough to the birds, so small resting places are built in the fields for the youngest and oldest members of the family to lounge around and hurl verbal abuse at the flying thieves. Sometimes a string of cans full of small stones is shaken to produce a staccato gravelly sound. But by far the most impressive sound is produced by the old farmer and his bull whip. Despite his fragility, the farmer swings the whip over his head, slowly at first and then cracks it with a retort like a pistol shot. The birds all scatter dutifully before regrouping in another field nearby.

In the middle of the field there is the sound of water everywhere. This is neither land nor water but a carefully constructed interface between the two. The first sign of an approaching rain storm is the surge of water through the canals, overflowing them and flooding the fields. The next sign is a sudden cool breeze blowing through; this indicates that the rain will arrive quickly. The frogs celebrate this flash flood with waves of croaking, little snakes slither around. Dragonflies dart back and forth, safe for the moment from the groups of children who enjoy hunting them. After the rain has passed, the children move stealthily through the fields with long slender sticks which have gobs of sticky material at their ends. If this material comes into contact with a speeding dragonfly it becomes a captive prize. It will be strung up with other victims and taken back to the kitchen to be fried as a snack.

Urban Water

As the water makes its way through the system and begins to enter the urban area, it starts to fragment as the fields become filled in and turned into housing developments. The water continues to flow through the urban area directed by larger and larger canals. Here it increasingly takes on qualities that are unknown in the rural environment. For example, water can flow in straight lines and intersect other canals at 90 degrees. This illustration shows such an intersection of two urban canals near downtown Denpasar. If the water passes a batik factory it can take on the surprising quality of being red color one day and blue the next.

Eventually, the remaining water filters through the city and down through the mangrove swamps on the southern coast, back to its source in the ocean.

Four views of the Uluwatu Temple

Kaja – Kelod Revisited

All water in Bali flows from the mountain to the sea, *kaja* to *kelod*. The image of the water's journey can be used to provide some insight into the meanings of these two Balinese terms introduced at the beginning of this chapter. For a Balinese person to move toward the mountain is to move towards clarity and holiness. The water held in these mountain lakes takes on these same characteristics. The lakes are considered to be mandalas and the water held in them takes on the very qualities of *kaja*: it is cool, quiet and clear.

As the water flows downward on its path to the ocean, moving towards *kelod*, it becomes increasingly fragmented and dispersed. It eventually reaches the ocean in a polluted state of dissipation and unpredictability. These qualities express the essence of *kelod*.

This image of *kaja-kelod* is neat and tidy. It is aesthetically appealing, and it might provide an insight into how the Balinese see their orientation to the world. But this common interpretation was turned upside down many years ago by one of Bali's most famous priests. His name was Danghyang Nirartha, a priest from Java who travelled to Bali and became one of Bali's most influential spiritual leaders. He looked out to the ocean and saw it in a different way.

Among his many contributions to Bali's cultural life were the series of temples he built, which now are some of the most revered on the island. One of these is Ulu Watu Temple. This temple sits at about the most *kelod* position that can be achieved in Bali, on the southwest coast of a peninsula on the southern tip of the mainland. The temple sits on a limestone promontory 100 metres above the Indian Ocean crashing and hissing below. The most immediate impression of this place is vast space, the sheer weight of all the air and expanse of water outwards to the horizon. It is said that Pedanda Nirartha achieved his final and complete enlightenment while praying at this temple, staring at the face of *kelod*. Following the common interpretation of *kaja-kelod*, one would assume that he would rather seek his final release from the foothills of Mount Agung while looking towards the summit of this great mountain. It is presumptive to ponder the thoughts of this venerated priest, but perhaps in his final contemplation of the vast, dark ocean he embraced the qualities of *kelod*. Perhaps he discovered in these unknown places not fear and dissolution, but freedom and liberation.

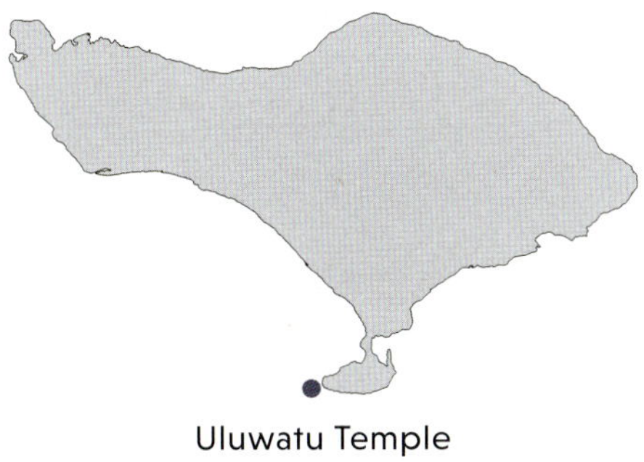

PART 03

VILLAGES

Self-Framing Settlements

In spite of the fact that Bali is a relatively small and self-contained place, it has never been a single unified state. Bali has always been a collection of smaller, competing kingdoms, either jostling and warring with each other, or making tentative attempts to cooperate. Throughout history, different kings have tried to exert their will over the entire island but these efforts were never successful.

The majority of the Balinese kingdoms developed in the fertile plains of the south. These kingdoms were the most glittering and lavish and have been most clearly noted in the historical record. Scattered between these kingdoms were hundreds of villages which enjoyed a rather autonomous relationship with the royal centers of power. These villages have always displayed the contrasting qualities of being royal dependencies on one hand, and on the other, independently minded and self-governing settlements.

In this map each of the green dots represents one village, and each red dot represents one of the nine major kingdoms in Balinese history. According to this map, there doesn't seem to be any special correlation between the villages and the kingdoms: the villages are not clustered around the kingdoms like satellites around centres of royal power. The location of the villages seems more influenced by Bali's topography, since they are found mostly in the lowlands and close to the coast. If they form any linear patterns, it is because they are following the course of a river. Each of the nine kingdoms is also located by a major river.

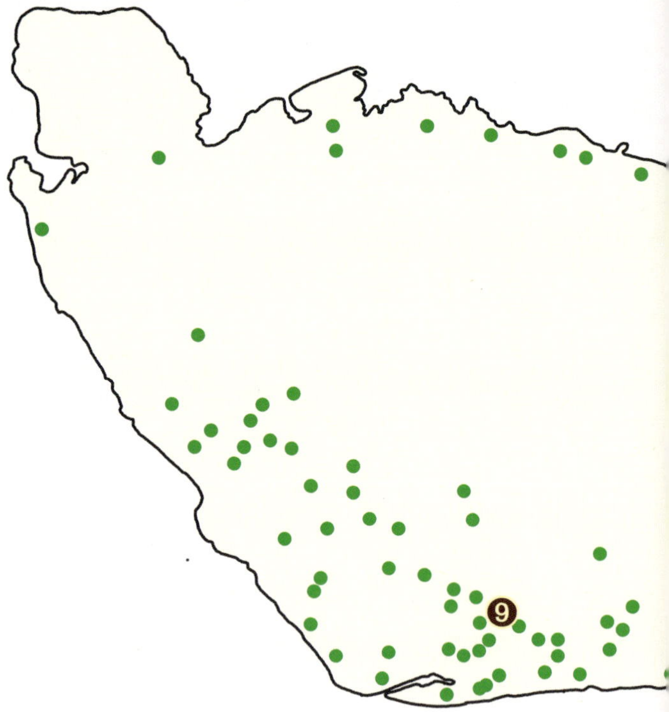

- ❶ Badung
- ❷ Tabanan
- ❸ Mengwi
- ❹ Gianyar
- ❺ Bangli
- ❻ Klungkung
- ❼ Karangasem
- ❽ Buleleng
- ❾ Negara

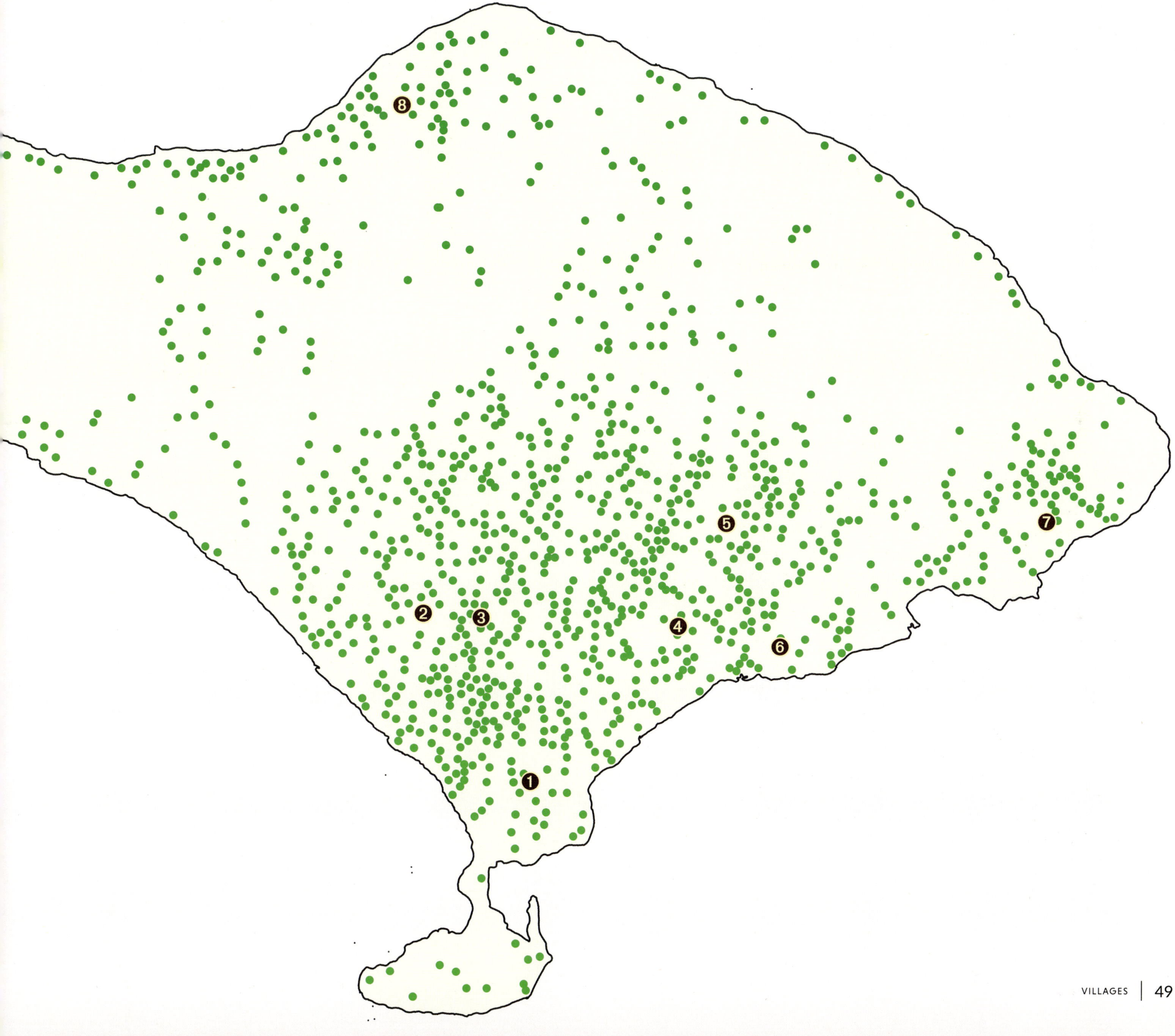
8
5
7
2
3
4
6
1

Mapping the Village. Big Trees

It is difficult to know exactly when you are entering the boundaries of a village. This is because there are several administration systems operating concurrently at the village level. They usually overlap each other, and it's easy to get your signals crossed. For example, a boundary marker for a village might appear in an empty field, or several different place names might be displayed on the same signboard at the same place.

There is one way, however, to know when you are entering or leaving a village. These boundaries are often marked by a large tree or a group of them. Except for the many radio towers now being built in Bali, and two or three bungee jumping towers in Kuta, these stately trees are the tallest objects in Bali. They can be helpful as landmarks in your travels. For example, if you are driving up a mountain through an empty area and approach a group of very tall trees you have most likely reached a graveyard, with an attendant temple called the Pura Dalem. This would be the most *kelod* place in the village. The trees here are sometimes partially scorched by cremation fires, but they remain robust and substantial. Despite their grand proportions, they are not here to be majestic or provide shelter. This is a frightening place, full of unseen forces, and most Balinese people wouldn't spend more time here than necessary.

This magnificent tree is located at a graveyard on the road between Tanah Lot and Kediri. People who drive past it will lightly sound their horns as a sign of respect and deference. A long look at this tree will show that its incredibly long branches are never really still but always swaying slightly, even if there seems to be no breeze. The local people call it 'Pohon Ujan' (Rain Tree). It is relatively rare and allowed to grow only in venerated spots as shelter for the spiritual beings believed to dwell there. The tree has its own priest and is particularly sacred as it stands over a graveyard exclusively as the final resting place for children under the age of two. But the local people feel there is no need to fear this place as long as they take the time to remember to pay homage to the unseen world they believe resides there.

Village Centre

It is at the village centre you will find the most inviting trees. Quite often a massive banyan tree will be growing here, with an unqualified invitation for any passer-by to enjoy the shade from its dense foliage; the temperature can actually be several degrees cooler in the depth of its shade. The tree at upper right is from the village of Buduk. The tree at lower right is found just north of the village of Kapal.

On the opposite page is a tree from the village of Blahkiuh, which pushed the limit of how large one of these magnificent trees could grow. It was visible for miles around and clearly marked the location of the village centre. One day it was toppled in a severe storm, and along with the tree the village itself became lost to view. Overnight, a place that was hard to miss became a place that was hard to find.

Village Centre

The centre of a classic south Bali village contains several common elements. Close by the banyan tree is often found a simply designed pavilion called a *wantilan*. These structures are surprisingly plain, lacking the ornamentation that adorns so much of Balinese life and thought. Traditionally, *wantilan* were made with wooden pillars and thatched roofs; these are now rare but still can be found in more secluded villages.

A *wantilan* is used for a variety of purposes. Temporary health clinics are set up to give the children vaccinations, and women gather here for afternoon aerobic classes. This is the place for ping-pong games, *gamelan* practice, or general relaxation. A *wantilan* is the village clubhouse.

Floor of a *wantilan* made from bricks, pillars of wood, South Central Bali.

Structures in rural Bali occasionally use living trees as structural elements. But these structures are usually small resting pavilions in the rice fields. To the left is a very unusual, much larger, meeting pavilion supported by 4 living trees (see the Vespa at the left corner), near the village of Payangan.

A *wantilan* is most lively and generates the most excitement when it is used as the site for a ritual cock fight, called *tajen*. With the exception of a few women selling snacks to the participants, this is a man's event, a time for social theatre and display. It is a fight to the death for the roosters and it allows men to experience warfare vicariously, allowing them to be warriors without actually having to go to war.

Champion fighting cock, South Central Bali.

Village Centre, Balé Kul-Kul

The final element that completes the classic south Bali village centre is a wooden drum tower, a *kul-kul*. If the *wantilan* is the meeting hall, the *balé kul-kul* is the public address system. Pounding on a wooden drum to communicate within a village is an ancient Southeast Asian tradition and is still used on a daily basis in Bali. The messages are sent through various patterns of drum beats; the intensity of the beating also adds emphasis to the message. Some messages are mundane, just calling the neighborhood men for a meeting at the *wantilan*. But some are more serious. If the banging on the drum is loud and urgent, this means there is an emergency, maybe a fire, maybe even thieves from a nearby village. For whatever this emergency might be, the men are expected to head to the crisis. In present days someone will make a call to the police office so a referee will be on hand if needed.

Both *wantilan* and *balé kul-kul* stand somewhat apart from the stricter canons of temple architecture and therefore have some more freedom in their design. Some of these structures become individualistic and even eccentric.

The example on the left is from Pura Penataran in the village of Suter near the rim of the Batur caldera. This simple architectural form is representative of smaller mountain villages. But even though they are simpler than the more grandiose examples in the south central cultural centres, this example shares the same ritual importance.

In the middle is an extremely rare five-sided *balé kul-kul*, one of three examples that are located along a road that runs north and south from the city of Tabanan up to the foothills of Mount Batukaru. This example is located in the village of Biaung. It is hard to imagine a more difficult challenge for the builders: was the architect expressing a spiritual revelation? Or perhaps he wanted to see if this form was possible to build, or maybe he simply wanted to create his masterpiece. On the right, this graceful architectural statement was located at one of Denpasar's busiest intersections.

It their efforts to weave in and out of the traffic, most drivers missed this beautiful tower. This was one building that deserved to be lifted up and set squarely in the centre of a quiet park so that people could enjoy its form. But all this must be written in the past tense because in 2011 this structure was demolished to make way for a more modern version.

Warung

In the village centre, and located throughout the village, are food kiosks called *warungs*, the places where most of the village socializing takes place. Each *warung* has its own identity; one is a favourite of the older folks who sit quietly and watch the village life go by, another is presided over by a woman who is a privy to all the local gossip (and knows how to embellish it effectively). Another *warung* is a local hangout for teenagers who meet there to flirt and fume with each other. Many *warungs* are known for their take-away food, which is often quite tasty. The *warung* illustrated on the left is from the village of Munduk, seen at four o'clock in the afternoon. The schools have just let out their students and there is a line of them waiting patiently for the owner to prepare her specialty, one plate at a time.

The *warung* on the right is from the harbour of Singaraja at noon, eerily empty.

Warungs are rarely well-built, they are usually tacked together, and taken as a whole they are a little shabby. Chickens and dogs wander through, unless ejected by a broom or a foot. But the ambience of a *warung* is surprisingly intimate. Under buzzing fluorescent lights on long rainy evenings, many confession, are heard here, lots of ribald jokes told, family secrets revealed, and marriages proposed.

Family Compounds

Each Balinese person feels deep roots to the place where he or she was born. Whether these memories are pleasant and idyllic, or dark and ominous, a Balinese person seems incapable of escaping their roots. From the day of their birth a new born baby is ritually tied to the family compound, and the culture continuously stresses the predominance of family and community. Until recently, the majority of Balinese people rarely strayed too far from their home village, except en masse with other members of the village to pray, perhaps at a distant temple. Childhood memories are therefore deep and vivid. For a middle-aged person from the southern part of the island, life in the family compound might be remembered like this—

Traditional South Bali rice barn.

“Still dark in the morning, hearing Father turn on the Mahabharata serial radio drama, at full volume sounding garbled and distorted from the transistor radio by his bed. At dawn walking through the rice fields down the steep hill to the river for a chilly morning bath, then filling up the plastic jug with spring water for the day's use. The smells from the kitchen, wood smoke from the fire, the chillies frying in oil, combine with the strangely sweet and pungent smells from the pig pens.

Working in the fields till mid morning and then returning home for a big meal and then a rest. Afternoons of strong tropical sun, the powerful sunlight illuminating common objects and making them seem monumental. Or endless afternoons of rain, sitting on the floor of a pavilion and trying to guess where everyone was by looking for their sandals in front of the other pavilions.

Later in the afternoon back to the fields for another work session, and finally back to the river for another meeting of the bathing club. Return home to prepare for afternoon offerings.

In the evening the compound door was closed as the darkness began to expose the sinister forces hiding in places both familiar and unfamiliar. The household chickens made exhausting leaps into the small tree in the compound to avoid being bothered by the dogs during the night. Gamelan music would float in, which temple was it from? Or is it a practice session from a neighbour? If the fields were wet, the chorus of crickets and frogs would mingle with the raspy sounds of the swaying coconut leaves. All forming an invitation to join the sleep world of strange juxtapositions and freely roaming spirits."

When our nostalgic person returns to the village for a ceremony or just to visit, he or she will find some changes. Father's little plastic transistor has become a massive stereo system, there might be a minivan in the garage. The nearby *gamelan* might be rehearsing for a contracted performance at a Nusa Dua resort. But even though the children of today will remember different particulars about their childhood, their memories will flow with the same rhythms and qualities as the generations before them.

Traditional South Bali kitchen.

North Balinese Kitchen

"Dadong Manis had become blind through old age but that didn't prevent her from keeping her kitchen clean. This room and the small veranda in front of it was the entirety of her world, and she left no part of it unattended. She would squat on the floor, sweeping with one hand and follow the broom with the other hand to make sure she hadn't missed anything. None of this was done for sympathy, it was simply her job to do.

Her granddaughter would come to visit and the elder woman would also use her hands to see how the girl was doing. She would first touch her hair to see if the girl was wearing it long or short these days. Then she would touch to girl's chest to see if she was becoming a woman yet. She would squeeze her slender arms hoping that the girl was putting some meat between her skin and bones.

Her husband was a surly man who scared his grandchildren. But he was devoted to his wife and was never too far away in case she had to admit she needed help with something. He was loyal to her throughout their lives together, and after she died he followed her quickly into death."

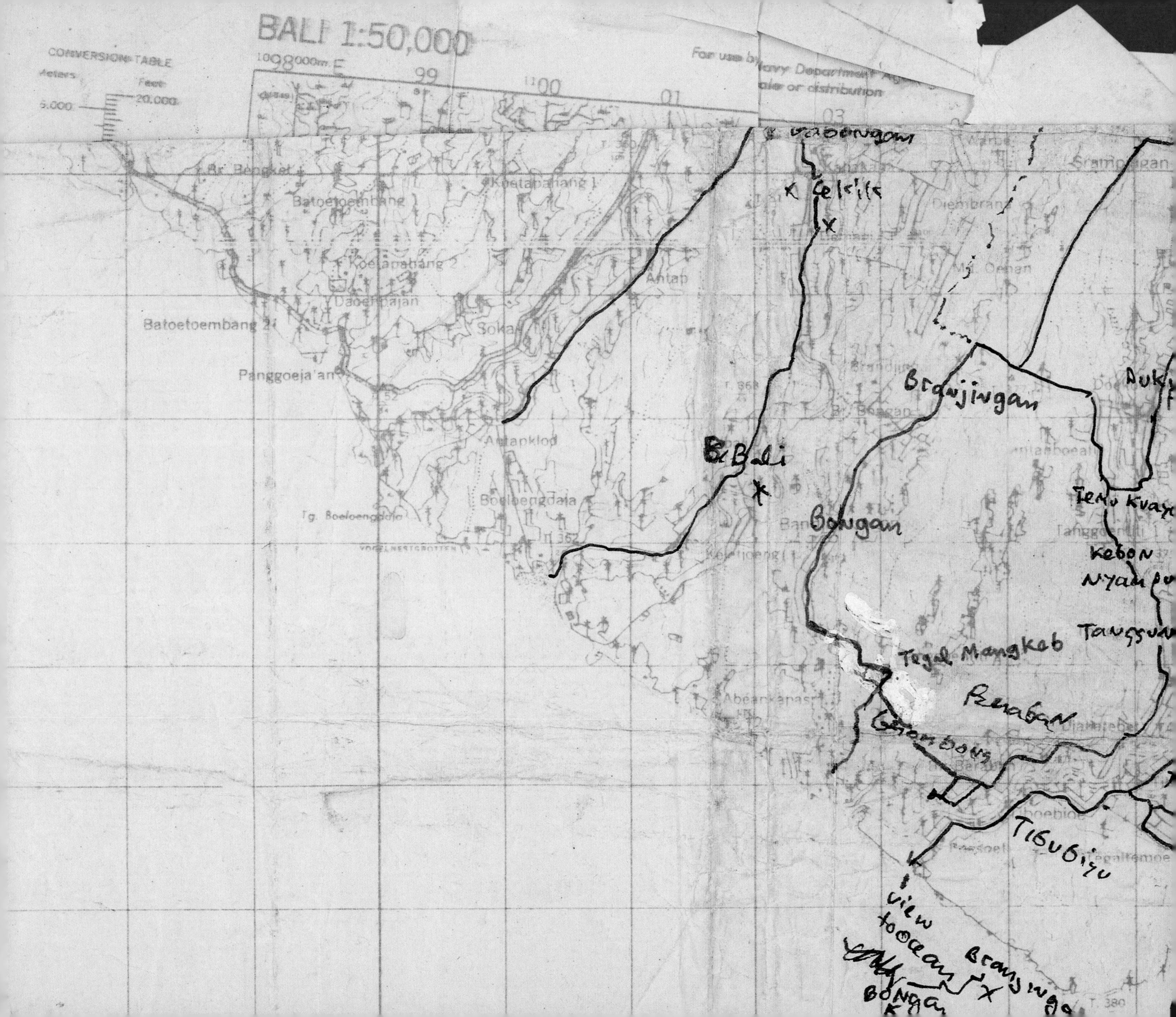

BALI 1:50,000
CONVERSION TABLE
Feet
20,000
Batoetoembang
Koelapabang 2
Batoetoembang 2
Panggoeja'an
Soka
Antap
Antapklod
Boeloengdaja
Tg. Boeloengdaja
Abeankapas
Celkik
Branjingan
Bali
Bongan
Tegal Mangkeb
Penaban
Kebon
Nyampu
Tibubiyu
view to ocean
BONGAN

Mambang
Sambunggede
Pelemgede
Lumajang
Samsam
Bale Agung
Tuak ilang
Baturiti
Tista
Kukuh
Belumbang
Deh Malet
Bantas
Bongan Gede
Bongan Tengah
Delod Puri

PART 04

MAPPING
THE BALINESE SOUL

❶ Gotong Royong

Sunday morning, 6:30 am. The wooden drum tower announces it is time to start: the local work detail is supposed to assemble at the *wantilan* for the morning's project. Some weeds need to be cleared from the side of the road. Five people could do the job but 25 are called to work. This is an example of mandatory manual labor in the village called "*gotong royong*". One purpose of this exercise is indeed to clear the brush, but an equally important reason is to get the people of the village working together on something. Solidarity is the key to the health of the village. If someone cannot turn up and help, they simply pay a small fee to the *banjar* as compensation. There always is a project that needs to get done, by both men and women, and they sometimes grumble about the time requested of them. But they also seem to enjoy the camaraderie of these sessions and would probably miss this socializing if this custom was eliminated.

Some steps in the process of making thatch. To the upper left, attaching the thatch to lengths of split bamboo. Lower left, the handmade rope used to tie up the thatch. To the right, one length of thatch ready to be trimmed and set on the roof.

One of the common *gotong royong* activities is to repair the communal structures of the village: walls need to be repaired and roofs replaced. The materials needed for this repair work is often close at hand. In the lowland plains of the south, wild grasses (*alang alang*) from the hillsides are used for thatching, and volcanic stone (*paras*) is used to for the walls. Women delve into the river to scoop up sand from the river bottom, and this sand is used to make cement. Medium-sized rocks are also found on the river banks, and rock gathering families trade in these small boulders. For villagers near to the ocean, broken bits of coral washed up on the beach can also be used in wall construction. Wood from coconut trees is commonly used for construction projects, and a stand of bamboo is never far away. This plant can be used for almost anything.

Roof tiles are often purchased from villages that specialize in producing them. Increasingly cement is becoming a standard building material. Its origin is far away in Java where huge cement factories provide for the Archipelago's construction needs.

❷ Alami

Needless to say, the activities of daily life in a traditional village give the people a close affinity to the natural world. But to call the Balinese 'earthy' would make this characteristic seem trite and cliché. Their bond to the earth is much deeper and more complex, and not at all sentimental. There is not much queasiness about the natural world: it is accepted all its aspects from soothing to jarring. From a Balinese perspective it would be considered 'earthy' to butcher a pig with your own hands. It would be even more 'earthy' to clean out the contents of the pigs intestines with your bare hands.

There is much respect paid to the power and wisdom that is available from the natural world. The term for being in tune with the working of the natural world is *"alami"*. A village priest once said that in former times Balinese people could do amazing things like fly through the air. He believed this was made possible because they went into the forest to gain knowledge. Now young people go to government schools and, according to him, this causes them to regress into ordinary humans.

This lack of sentimentality extends to the taking of life too. Butchering livestock is an integral part of life on Bali. Sometimes a prayer is said on behalf of the animal to help its soul find a better place in the next world. But after this spiritual moment the pig's death is horrific: it is gorged in the neck with a knife and bled to death. This method of processing pork has received much comment from visitors to Bali, but these observers may not have seen how the pigs lived their lives before they died.

The luckiest pigs are free to wander around in an open area of the family compound called *tebe*. They move so slowly that sometimes chickens ride on their backs for some slow motion entertainment. Other pigs are tethered to a small tree where they either eat or sleep. The meals are not bad, freshly cooked banana tree soup with cassava leaves. Other pigs are raised in open-air concrete pens, given daily baths and eat the same cuisine.

One Night Under a Marbled Sky, The Pig's Souls were sent Aloft

"Soon after midnight they were carried into the courtyard tied to long bamboo poles and layed on the ground in parallel rows. The man designated as the butcher paused a moment before plunging his knife in to the neck artery of each pig. One by one they were butchered as other men held their screaming contorted bodies, the blood pulsating out of the neat round holes under their eyes. This blood was collected into tin bowls to be used later. After the pigs were motionless their bodies were splashed with kerosene and set alight to singe off the body hair. The pigs were then butchered systematically, no part was discarded. The process was like an anatomy lesson, all the parts were separated and minced up on banana leaves laid on the ground. Some men sat for hours cutting up aromatic spices, other men roasted coconut and then grated it. Eventually the meat was lightly cooked and mixed together with the other ingredients. Finally the blood, now thick and darkened, was poured over the mixture and worked in by hand. It was almost dawn and our breakfast was now ready."

Carved ornament from family temple,
Mas village, South Central Bali.

❸ Ramé

Another aspect of life in Bali is the predilection for density, a love of busy-ness. This quality is called *"ramé"* and is greatly enjoyed. The Balinese tend to be restless and look for any kind of project to occupy themselves. There doesn't seem to be much Zen-like appreciation for emptiness; a bare wall is seen as an unfinished project. A cultural aversion to emptiness (in either thought or action) is reflected in the saying that if you stare into space (*bengong*) a demon will enter your mind.

The effort given towards filling space is often much more than is necessary from a utilitarian point of view. Things are rarely done in the easiest or fastest way, and done by choice, not because of poor planning. One visible consequence of this tendency is the ornamentation that graces architectural forms. The walls, gateways, and doors of temples and houses are favorite targets for the energies of artisans. These surfaces more often than not end up bristling with complex designs of shape and color.

Paras stone carving detail, Pule Temple,
Mas village, South Central Bali.

❹ Nongkrong

All this activity creates a sort of psychic density that is felt by most Balinese—the atmosphere feels thick and loaded. Try to take a simple stroll down a village street and you will find that this is not possible. As you meet various people along this road you will be asked:

"Where are you going?
Who will you see there?
What is in your bag?
Mangoes? What kind of mangoes?
Where did you buy them?
How much did you pay? Really!! So much!"

And then the next day on the other side of the village you meet someone you haven't seen for weeks who says:

"You really paid too much for those mangoes…"

A walk through a village is a promenade across the theatre of the present moment, with full audience watching you perform. This popular type of social theater is called *"nongkrong"*.

If you drive into a village at around 5pm you need to prepare yourself for the reception committee: the street will be lined with spectators. The best strategy is to embrace the possibilities and play with them a bit. Even if you are driving a beat-up old Vespa coughing out blue smoke, you can still make a good impression. You can sit up straight and tall with a half smile on your face, acknowledging (slightly) those people you wish to notice. You can become a conquering general returning from battle.

Sketches of a dance rehearsal,
Batuan Village, South Cenreal Bali.

❺ Nakal

One element in this generalized look at Balinese culture concerns the elusive meaning of good and evil. From the classic western understanding of this dichotomy, these two terms have clear values attached to them: 'good' should defeat and subjugate 'evil'. By contrast, in the Balinese world view both these qualities are an integral and constant aspect of life, not the starting point for a crusade. Good and evil will always be around, they will always be in conflict, neither will be able to defeat the other. One can only hope to achieve an uneasy equilibrium between the two.

Balinese people are aware of these two forces inside themselves and do their best to reconcile their dual roles of being saints and sinners. But they don't miss the chance of having some fun along the way, playing one side off the other. Both opportunism and naughtiness can be used at the right time and in the right degree to earn a certain amount of cultural respect. A parent will often call their child *"nakal"* with a clear note of pride in their voice. Naughtiness in children (especially boys) is seen as a sign of creativity. But this extends beyond children. Even adults who are engaged in nefarious activities can be called *nakal*. In effect this minimizes the seriousness of the offence.

Beyond Nakal

At a deeper level, the distinction between good and evil begins to lose its coherence. There is a feeling that things are neither bad or good, they just exist. The Balinese tend to confirm things as they see them:

The man has a drooping jaw
The child has a leaky eye
The monkey is urinating of the floor
The man next door is throwing up so loudly that the dogs are barking at him

There is not a strong judgmental aspect in these observations. It doesn't matter greatly if they are good or bad, the important thing is how strongly they are felt.

A dancer of great skill will mesmerize the audience with his or her movements and leave an indelible impression. A famous Arja dancer's eyes flash like she is about to explode. But in the end it is not about the dance tradition or the dancer's eyes, it is about the strength of the moment. You might see a tightly-packed crowd on the street, drawn by either a traffic accident or a thief who has been caught. The people watching this scene are not trying to see something awful, it is simply the power of the event that is irresistible. There were lines of people who scaled the outer walls of Sanglah hospital to see the mutilated bodies of the victims of the first Bali bombings. Their motivation was to be struck by the power of the scene. The realisation of the horror of this event and the wider implications of this nightmare came later.

With this wide-open approach to life comes the licence to find humour everywhere. It is understood that the object of this laughter cannot get angry, the humour is just being aimed at something plain to see and is therefore self-evident. There is no reason to deny it or get angry.

❻ Niskala

Another aspect to Balinese belief is that there is yet another universe unfolding concurrently along with the world we can see. It is a vast place that has its own architecture and is inhabited by a rambunctious and unruly crowd. It is a realm of existence invisible to our normal vision and can be perceived only at certain times and in specific ways. But in spite of this elusiveness, the world is believed to have a profound effect on the daily lives of the Balinese people.

This is the abode of the spirits and spiritual energy called *"niskala"*. There are believed to be different forms of spirits here residing in different places. They embody a wide range of forms and characteristics that find parallels in the human world. Some are the souls of deceased family members who occupy different levels of this world, depending of their degree of liberation from the material world. There are ghouls that annoy, along with unspeakable monsters who can cause paralysis or even death. There are guardian spirits that accompany the newborn through its birth and first days of life. These spirits eventually become quite naughty and bother the child in minor ways. They are then asked to leave the child in a small ceremony. There are beings who are believed to cross back and forth between the world of daily life and the spirit world. They might be disgruntled or trapped by their circumstances, which causes them to retaliate using invisible means.

Great efforts are used to appease these spirits. There are many spiritual mediums who are in tune with the workings of the invisible world. People can employ these mediums to get information about an unusual sickness or unfortunate occurrence, or to placate an especially troublesome spirit.

Night time view of Pura Beji, Bongan village, Tabanan Regency, Bali

1
2
3
4

Dealing With Niskala

Balinese discuss these matters constantly amongst themselves, but only in a whisper when others are within earshot. They are fully aware that these types of mystical beliefs are not widely shared by people from outside their island, at least from the mainstream of technological cultures. The Balinese don't want to be laughed at for beliefs they feel strongly about, neither do they want to be patronized or considered naïve. The coexistence of the spiritual world and the empirical world seems perfectly acceptable to the vast majority of Balinese people. A school principal might pride himself on his ability to implement the latest pedagogical techniques with his students. The same educator might return home and chat with family and friends about the details of various types of spirits that could be encountered on a day to day basis—a different type of education, but equally important to him.

Visitors to Bali who consider themselves secular people need to come to terms with Balinese spirituality, beliefs that run counter to the traditions of rational humanism. One common strategy for these visitors is to re-frame the Balinese spirit world in psychological terms, to define the spirits as manifestations of unconscious fears and desires. In many ways it seems like common sense, forward-thinking and modern. It is also arrogant.

Psychology is a relatively new school of thought and its precepts are still evolving. Some anthropological field work was done in the 1930's by Margaret Mead and Gregory Bateson using Freudian analysis to unravel the Balinese psyche. This seemed very modern at the time. But now that the schools of psychology have developed and grown, the idea that there is an id and an ego floating around in our consciousnesses itself seems mechanistic and simplistic. The psychological models we use to 'explain' Balinese spirituality will eventually be replaced by newer and newer models, each one calling the earlier one obsolete.

In the end it must be admitted that the intellectual beliefs of the western world are constructs that evolve and change, and are no less fabrications than the spiritual beliefs of the Balinese. Has there been any human model of reality that has reached perfect understanding? All of our systems of belief to help us understand the incomprehensible qualities of life are destined to fall short, from whatever culture one might come from.

Rather than trying to determine the rightness or wrongness of a culture's beliefs, it would be more constructive to see how well these beliefs work on a daily basis. How useful are they in running a culture? Do they empower their members or do they obstruct them? Do these beliefs create a society that is sustainable, or will it spend its energy and wear itself out? One way to come to terms with Balinese spirituality is how successful it is in giving meaning and dimension to Balinese life. And beyond that, to just respect the depth of the mystery of life and leave it unknowable.

Using this methodology it is possible to identify a danger inherent it Balinese spirituality. Some Balinese feel that the spirit world can be used as a tool that can be manipulated, used as a shortcut to a desired goal. Why go through the lengthy process of learning and growth required to make a powerful work of art, when you can go to a spirit medium and have the whole thing arranged for you? It is a fairly easy matter to get some magic put on your paintings to make them sell. At

the same time (and from the same practitioner) you can get the opposite magic put on your competitor's paintings so they won't sell. It is also easier to explain a death caused by a rapid and mysterious illness as a curse sent by a disgruntled in law, than to admit that your kitchen is filthy. Love potions are popular, there are many methods to guaranteed to bring you rapid wealth. The misuse of spirituality is a slippery slope and the use of black magic in the end tends to harm most the person who uses it.

There is a certain type of spirit called a *leyak*. The belief is that *leyak* originate as people who have learned the methods to transform themselves into a variety of malevolent creatures, and then to disappear into the air. Often a *leyak* enters a person when a person is dreaming and tried to harm him or her. The fear caused by one of these dreams is enough to immobilize the dreamer.

One characteristic of a *leyak* dream is that this spirit (usually translated as witch) won't let the dreamer wake up to end the ordeal. As the witch commits the foulest of deeds (like eating the child of the dreamer), the victim tries to wake up but the witch grabs him or her by the throat and refuses to let go. The sobs of such a dreamer in the middle of the night start slowly and softly but soon become emphatic, plaintive moans. It doesn't take long for the other people in the house to guess what is happening; the dreamer is awoken and calmed enough to tell the story of the dream. There will usually be a late night call back to the village to make sure everyone in the family is all right.

❼ Paling

In this dense and finely tuned society it is easy for things to get confused and go off course. This feeling of disorientation is called *"paling"*.

There always is the possibility that life in Bali can suddenly lose its coherence, and the feeling of balance can be lost. The enjoyable dense and lively atmosphere of ramé can become claustrophobic and oppressive. The theatrical quality of life, *nongkrong*, turns into cheap theatrics and over-acting. The pleasure of being a bit of a brat, *nakal*, becomes licence to do whatever one damn well pleases. The acceptance of both the good and bad in one's life degenerates into a defeatist fatalism. The deep and mature mysticism of Bali becomes mere magic. The spirit of mutual assistance, *gotong royong*, becomes a conspiracy to hold down individuals that try to reach too high.

Group solidarity becomes vigilantism and there can be violence between woman and men or between adults and children. A simple glance can be seen as an indictment. One man prays to get some quick cash, a woman prays that the younger woman who stole her husband will die in childbirth.

Balinese culture gives its members ample opportunity to dig their own graves, and some people do just that.

Temple statue, North Bali

Living in the Mind of God.

Bhuwana Agung Bhuwana Alit is one of the two aspects of the Balinese thought-world that provide a way to navigate out of the cultural congestion described in this chapter. The concept known as *Bhuwana Agung Bhuwana Alit*, literally translates into, 'big world small world'; essentially it refers to a macrocosmos-microcosmos dichotomy. There are very subtle and esoteric interpretations of this concept (Lansing), but the most common, day to day understanding is that each person is an identical copy of the universe in miniature. Each of us contains all the elements of the world at large, only on a vastly smaller scale. We are all fragments, and therefore participants of a larger entity.

All this might seem too abstract to have much of an effect over daily life, but it has a powerful effect on the pattern of daily life on Bali. This concept helps blur the distinctions between the self and the world outside. The feeling of 'otherness' and alienation to the outside world is diminished or even eliminated. What's more, it is difficult to even explain the concept of alienation to a Balinese person, the concept is so unusual for them.

One consequence of this unity between inside and outside is that a person's sense of space becomes infinitely large. When a person gets too crowded he or she can turn to the universe for some relief. It's not the case that someone will feel larger than themselves, they actually do become larger than themselves.

What an amazing opportunity to have the entire universe to wander around in! All the good and bad, sweet and sour, all the complexity of the universe in each and every one of us. Inexhaustible opportunities and possibilities.

The image of Bhuwana Agung Bhuwana Alit shows the world in all its unity, and importantly it shows how it all works together—how all these separate and sometimes contradictory elements of life can harmonize and work together as a coherent whole.

Tri Hita Karana is a related concept that works in tandem with *Bhuwana Agung Bhuwana Alit*. This concept expresses three forms of harmony: between humanity and nature, within humanity itself, and between humanity and the spirit world. The main function of *Tri Hita Karana* is to balance all aspects of life, with the goal of achieving awareness and inner peace.

There is one way that a Balinese person can form a deeper understanding of these two concepts and that is through the traditions of offering making, and the placement of these offerings in domestic spaces, as well as in temples. Offerings are used every day, from simple canang sari (as shown above), to more complex offerings for auspicious days, and even offerings that involve the efforts of the entire Bali Hindu population.

There are two functions performed by offerings. The first is simply the communal collaborative effort to make them. The simple offerings can be made at home, either alone or with family, friends, or with neighbors. Even at this level, the offerings are being used as a special form of collective activity, that creates a spirit of oral learning as daily practice (162 Andrea Acri & Michele Stephen).

The second way is more esoteric and so detailed that there are not many Balinese people who are able to fully understand or explain them. This is the realm of the high priests; they have the ability to find the source of this knowledge in the ancient Javanese written texts and mantras. In simple terms, offerings can be seen as mandalas that are seen as maps of the spirit world. They give form to the invisable abode, and provide a way for the Balinese to enter, and navigate through *Bhuwana Agung Bhuwana Alit* and *Tri Hita Karana*. These two concepts help the Balinese remember who they are, and how they are supposed to live.

PART 05

RITUALS OF IDENTITY

Pura Desa Batuan, Central Bali.

What a Temple is

There is a saying that Bali is the land of 10,000 temples; other people estimate the number at 100,000. It all depends how you count. For our purposes it is enough to say that you can find some kind of temple nearly everywhere in Bali. They are inside and outside of homes and businesses, at dams, at irrigation networks, under big trees, next to unusually shaped rocks. Here we focus on the village temples because these are the locations where people meet to enact their rituals of identity. The temples have a fairly basic layout. Simply put, they are a series of walled courtyards which contain a variety of shrines. From our point of view, temples can be thought of as theatre stages where the human and spirit worlds meet and interact. During a temple ceremony, the members, through prayer, invite the Gods to descend so they can be praised and entertained. The Gods in turn speak through spirit mediums to give advice or criticism, to correct those things that have become distorted. Temples create the spaces for these interactions to unfold; the temple courtyards become the focus for these meetings to occur. Seeing temples as the context for spiritual interaction shows how beautifully appropriate they are for their purpose. Some temples have courtyards that are large and expansive; others are small and intimate. But essentially Balinese temples are empty spaces; their meaning comes from the people who animate them. The shape and size of a temple varies widely throughout the island. They can be simple isolated shrines in mountainous areas, or carefully placed courtyards along the ridges of hills, twisting down through dramatic valleys. In the wide open rice growing areas, the temples are more generous with their spaces, sometimes growing to grandiose and baroque proportions. The temples at the beaches are more mysterious and sometimes downright frightening.

Portrait of a Temple

The Pura Desa is the principal temple of a typical Balinese village. It constitutes the ritual and social centre of the community. It is generally situated at the very heart of the village, or at a prominent crossroads

Upper right, Pura Desa Ubud seen from across the street. Lower right the same temple, aerial view.

1. Jaba
2. Kori Agung
3. Jeroan
4. Taring
5. Gedong Penyimpenan
6. Padmasana
7. Meru
8. Paruman
9. Gedong Ratu Lingsir
10. Candi Bentar

Puri Kerobokan Central Bali.

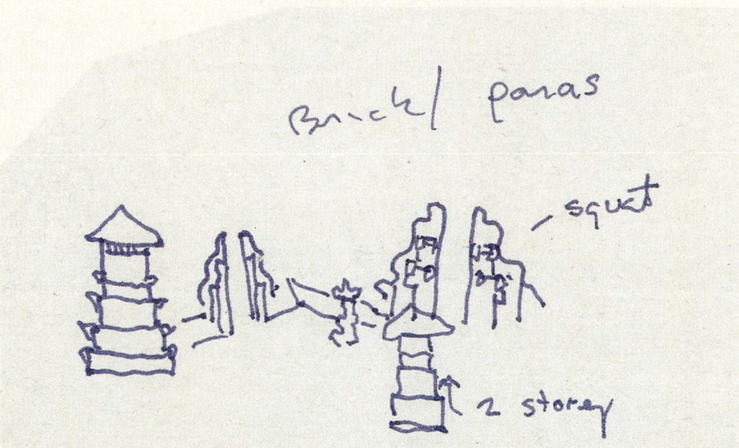

Field notes, Ubud South Central Bali.

Pura front gate, Kuwum, Mengwi.

How a Temple is Formed

As already mentioned, the shapes of the temple are created by its walls and gateways. Even though these architectural elements are mainly to serve utilitarian purposes, they are also irresistible targets for the restless energy of Balinese artists. Some main gates grow to sizeable proportions and become like the proscenium arch that frames a theatre stage. The walls are often filled with carved ornamentation, sometimes long narrative panels.

Door gate, Pura Griya Sakti,
Manuaba village, Central Bali.

Main Gate, Tirta Empul complex,
Tampak Siring, Bali.

How a Temple is Used

As mentioned before, there is no standard arrangement for a temple. So to explain its system of courtyards we will focus on one particular temple, Pura Geria Sakti from the village of Kendaran in south central Bali. This is one of the grand temples in Bali that is associated with the famous priest from the 14th Century, Pedanda Nirartha and is the clan temple for the venerable Manuaba clan. This temple clearly exhibits the progression from the first to the third courtyard. It shows how the courtyards guide the visitors in the lowest, most common, areas, through a series of stairs and gateways into the holiest part of the temple.

During a temple ceremony the activity in the lowest courtyard (being the most *kelod* area of the temple) is called "**Jaba**", a place for vaudeville style entertainment, sometimes bawdy, sometimes profane. There are food and drink *warungs*, sometimes places for petty gambling, the most secular dances are performed here. This is also the place where blood sacrifices are performed for the ground spirits.

Starting from here the direction is towards *kaja*, towards the mountain, towards the inner courtyard, towards an increasingly spiritual experience. The middle courtyard, "**Jero Tengah**", is where the worshippers wait for their turn to bring their offerings to the priests; it is a sort of staging area. At the height of the ceremonies there can be long lines of people waiting; there are plenty of opportunities for people watching and small talk. But the relatively free-wheeling attitude of the lower courtyard is not evident here. Already, the people's attention is directed to the inner courtyard, where there is not only physical conformity to custom and dress, but also an expectation that a person's thoughts and feelings should be acceptable to the gods in attendance.

The inner sanctum is called "**Dalem**", or "**Jeroan**", and it is the final stop. In this particular temple, the entire inner courtyard is blessed by an enormous banyan tree growing immediately behind the holiest shrine. This massive tree and its thick foliage transforms the sunlight into a soft glow of cool green light.

Moving from south to north, (*kelod* to *kaja*), is the *wantilan* and *balé kul kul*.

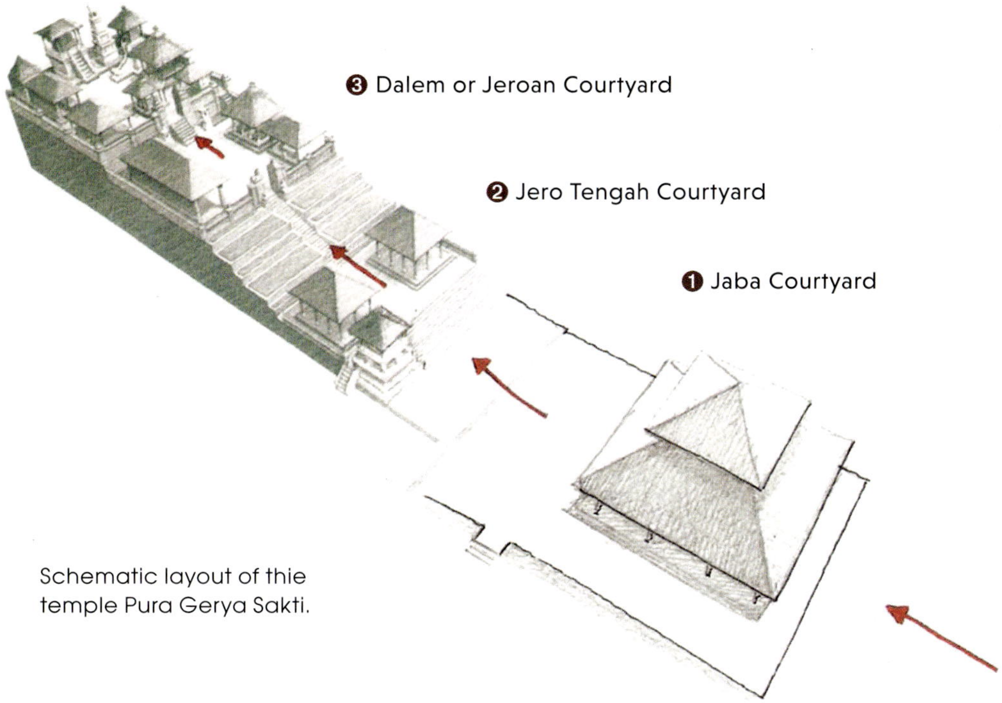

Schematic layout of thie temple Pura Gerya Sakti.

❶ In the outer courtyard, or Jaba.

❷ Stairway to middle courtyard, Jero.

❷ In the middle courtyard with split gate entrance to the inner courtyard.

❸ The inner most courtyard, or Dalem.

Shrines and Pavilions

Located within the inner courtyard of the temple are the various shrines which are the focus of the temple ceremony. Each shrine has a specific connection to a specific place, clan, or deified ancestor. Taken as a whole, they embrace the entire pantheon of Balinese spirituality with its rich webs of networks. The shrines are a way to see how the temple relates to the various concerns and activities of the village, and how the temple's congregation is connected to other temple groups around the island. Some of the smaller shrines show the more obscure links between temples that might not be known to the average member; this knowledge is the privilege and responsibility of the temple's priests.

The most basic pavilions are called "*gedong*", these have the important utilitarian function of storing the sacred objects that are revered by the village. During the ceremony these venerated objects are taken out and displayed in other shrines called "*paruman*".

Paruman Pura Desa Sebatu.

Village *wantilan* (community hall)

Meru

Meru shrines are the most visible, and the easiest to identify. The number of roofs reflects the importance of the ancestor it is dedicated to. There can be 3, 5, 7, 9, or 11 roofs which symbolize the various levels of the spiritual worlds in the Balinese cosmology. The more roofs a *meru* has is an indication of its importance.

Other than its spiritual function, a *meru* possesses true aesthetic beauty. Its elegance has become an emblem that represents the whole of Balinese architecture.

Unidentified *meru*, South Central Bali

Unidentified *meru*, working drawing, Central Bali.

Pura Pule Mas village,
South Central Bali.

Unidentified shrine, returning to nature. South Central Bali.

Pura Besakih, Central Bali.

Padmasana

The most important shrine in a temple complex is the "*Padmasana*". This is the seat of the God who is believed to become manifest during the temple ceremony. Most of these shrines have only one seat; very rarely they have multiple seats. At the temple complex called "*Besakih*" there is a magnificent *Padmasana* that has three seats. These shrines are located at the most "*kaja kangin*" point, and so most auspicious position in the temple.

Pura Sada, Kapal village, Central Bali.

Unique Variations

As mentioned before in this series, there is a good amount of freedom that each village has to establish their own particular ritual life. Most villages don't deviate too much from a 'standard' way of doing things, but occasionally you can find something unique.

Pictured above is a group of shrines located in a temple called *Pura Sada*. This is a very old temple, perhaps dating from the year 830AD, and is linked to the royalty of Mengwi.

As seen above, there are three main shrines standing guard over 54 small ones. It is said that this group of shrines is intended as a memorial to fallen soldiers from distant wars.

Top illustration, *'Meditation Chamber, Goa Gajah'*. Bottom left and right, *'A pair of statue fragments, Pura Desa Batuan'*

Statues and Carving

Temple walls often contain long carved reliefs that tell the stories of ancient myths or local folklore. There are selections from the mighty epics, the Mahabhrata and Ramayana, tales of bravery and intrigue. Sometimes the carvings contain small jokes, supplied by the artisans who may have been trying to entertain themselves during the long hours of work. There are even scenes that are explicitly erotic, but these are very rare.

Statues are found everywhere in a temple, both inside and outside, and especially at the entrance. These are the cast of characters that give life to the Balinese literary and spiritual traditions. The most venerable statues, called "*Pratima*", are placed in protective shrines in auspicious positions; some of these Pratima are hundreds of years old. Other statues stand at the entrance of the temple to either welcome or frighten the visitors. Still others become part of the architecture, as pillars or corner stones. Some statues are small and intimate, while others are monumental constructions. But all of them put a recognizable face on an unseen and abstract world.

These statues are the work of anonymous artists who did their work as a service to the community "*ngayah*" or for a very low daily stipend. Either way this work was not done to gratify the artist's egos, but rather in the spirit of community service.

Originally, these two statues on the left were painted with bright colours. Due to the humid climate, different coloured moss and lichens have added their earth tones to the mix.

This pair of statues is from the Pura Dalem, village of
Ayunan, close to Mengwi, South Central Bali.
2 examples from the Pura Desa,
Batuan village. South Central, Bali.

Ngayah

There are many preparations required for a temple ceremony. These preparations can involve several days of work, even weeks of activity by scores of people. This type of voluntary work for the temple is called *ngayah* and is a special form of *gotong royong*. After all the temporary structures are built and in place, it has been ritually activated.

Wayang Wong dance rehearsal, field drawing
Tejakula Village, North Bali,

Dance

There are other preparations besides preparing the temple grounds, other important elements of ritual life that can take years to develop and perfect. This is the music and dance that will accompany the temple activities. Most of the musicians and dancers are from the village itself, sometimes outside artists are invited to help out but this is unusual. In daily life these artists work as farmers, hotel employees, housewives and students. During the temple ceremony they transform themselves into the heroes of legend; Arjuna, Sita, Rama, and Panji. After the performance these players return to their normal routines and blend back into the rhythms of daily life.At first exposure to Balinese dance, one is overwhelmed with the sensations: the glittering costumes, the explosive music, the highly refined yet expressive movements. There are quiet moments too, but even when a dancer has paused into a still position he or she seems to be on the verge of bursting into the next passage.

A typical dance is composed of a long series of movements, each having its own name and classification, each with its own beginning and end. All these discrete movements are strung together like beads on a string, altogether forming the complete dance. If you watch a good dancer you will see that there is nothing missing, nothing is indistinct in the fluidity of the movements. Each one an episode in itself, each one connecting to the next. Becoming a dancer requires years of study, usually beginning in childhood. Many children enjoy studying dance; neighborhood dance classes are very popular and well attended.

At these chaotic mass lessons, the teachers can see who will excel. In the midst of the rambunctious children, one girl stands out, maintaining her concentration through the long series of movements. Sweating profusely she moves without embellishment, her focus unwavering.

Some of these students will go on to be accomplished dancers, others will learn just to fill in the roles to complete the temple ceremony. But each participant is a necessary part of the ceremony, all the roles need to be filled.

Dance performance, Field drawing,
Batuan village South Central Bali.

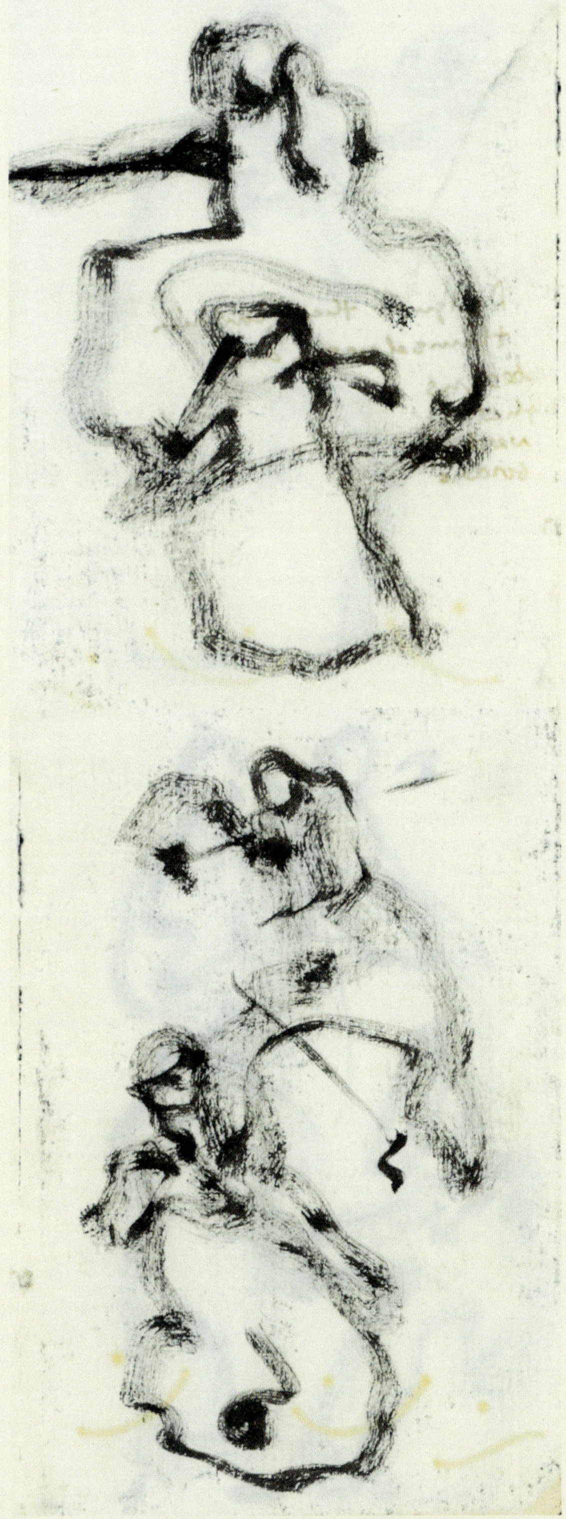

Dance performance, Field drawing,
Ubud village, South Central Bali,

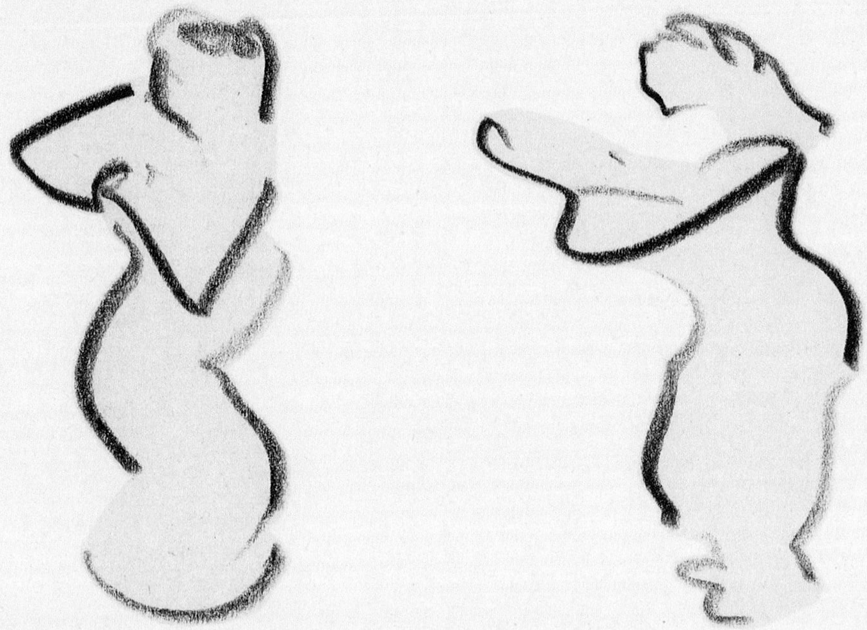

Dance rehearsal, field drawing, Batuan village.

Dancer from Gerih village demonstrates two different hand positions.

Music

The music of the *gamelan* is an equally rich and complex tradition. Like dance, it makes itself accessible to a variety of skill levels. There are roles for those who have become expert, and there are places for someone else who just wants to hit a gong. It is a user-friendly orchestra.

If dance is a series of related movements, music is a series of related cycles. *Gamelan* music can be written out as a sequence of numbers, which is in fact one way this music is taught. The different sequences of the music are written as strings of numbers on a blackboard in the *wantilan* where the music is rehearsed. Deliberate and stately musical passages end in a rich gong, and then stretch out into a different rhythm and speed altogether. The music is complex and multilayered; at the same time you can hear sharpness and honey, a flowing field full of sparks. The two drummers are the leaders of the ensemble. Tight and businesslike, they link together into an interlocking pattern of sound that pulls the *gamelan* along.

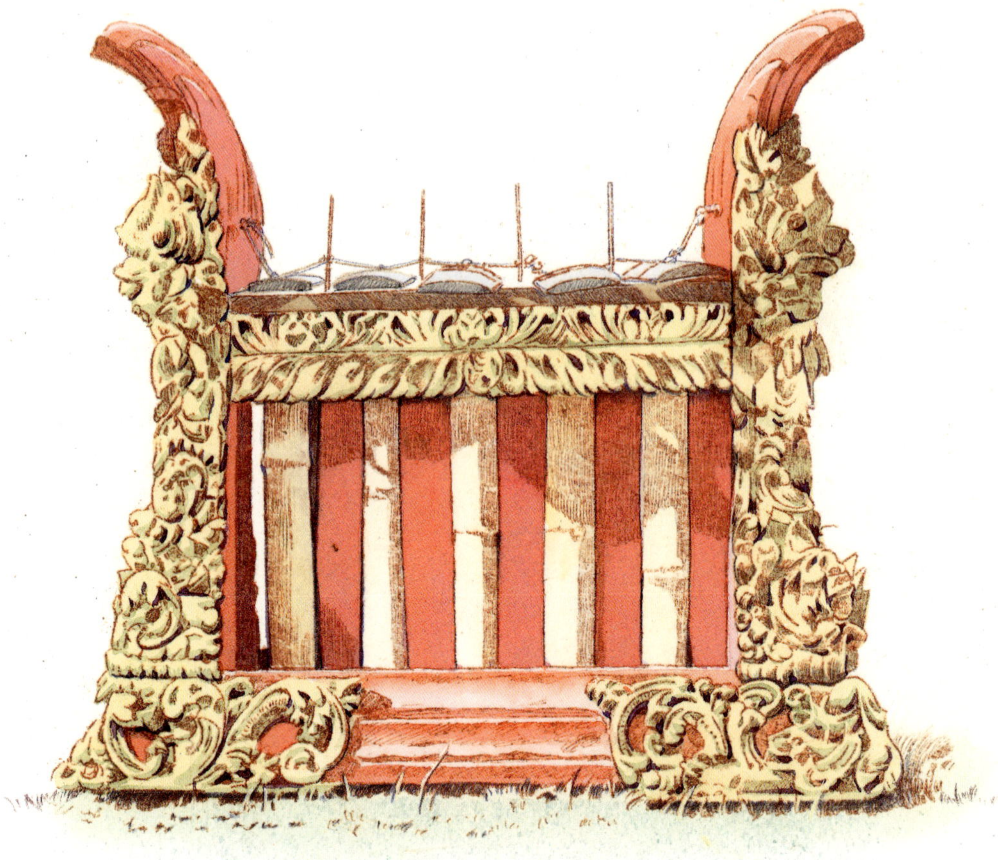

Gamelan instrument, Bali Art Center Denpasar.

Various Gamelan Musicians, field drawings.

The Stage is Ready, Its Time to Begin

"Sitting in the warung outside the temple, watching the parade and carnival. Some people in full temple dress sparkling with gold thread, others in T-shirts and jeans. A man sells sate, other men drink beer and gamble on little coloured wooden shapes. An old man spits out beetle juice, red and thick, two dogs lock in mortal combat.

Walk through the main gate and marvel at the breadth of the human imagination, curvilinear swirling forms carved into stone and brick, bamboo structures that will only last a few weeks, flamboyance and disregard. But this is no place to ponder aesthetics, this place is full of people chattering away, and watching each other. There are shifting waves of smiles and stares.

Some men are walking around with spears getting ready for a warrior dance, women sweep the ground. There is a tourist shooting a video, an elderly man drifts off to sleep. People are watching each other, teasing, flirting. Young women wearing translucent blouses, young men trying to be heroic. Some women compare the worth of their neighbour's gold jewellery, a man is doing his best to conceal a simmering rage. Everyone is a peer, everyone is on stage, there is no audience here.

The loosely grouped gamelan snaps to attention after the first bright hammered note, a distinct point of sound in the muggy air. The gamelan is aloft along with the incense and checkered cloth. The musicians stare off into unknown places as they play, the drummer's smile shows a perfect series of teeth, it becomes a white line across his place.

A flurry of silk and black hair animates the main door of the gate. A dancer glides from one spot to another without any hesitation or doubt, energy leaking out through her fingers, changes drift across her face. Young Kadek has become a feisty dancer. She and the musicians are locked together like drivers in heavy traffic, squeezing passion through a sieve of tradition and restraint.

Join the current of people into the inner courtyard and gaze upon the psychedelic enthusiasm of the offerings and decorated shrines. Chemical pink mixes with olive green, the air full of ancient chants forced through inadequate sound systems. The lightheadedness caused by wearing too many layers of clothing under the tropical sun. Even the unstable neighbour looks respectable with his granddaughter dozing in his lap. The people sweat and their skin is cool to the touch. We are all riding an aural highway of sound, much too loud and just about right at the same time. It would be foolish to resist. Best to let yourself be carried along.

By 6pm the clouds turn to pink, and by 8pm the people are starting to get tired. It has been a long day, a long week. A priest yawns wide and slow without trying to conceal it. Most of the people have gone home now, they have done what is required of them. A core group remains to complete the ritual and will receive the full benefit of it. These people are the inner circle of the greater vehicle. Suddenly the wash of sound, the music and the chants, the aural highway we have been riding all day stops abruptly. There is a startling silence, expansive and vast. After a few moments the priests begin to ring their bells again, each of them with a slightly different rhythm and pitch. They create a jumble of sound, just like the sounds of today, but now transformed into something small and delicate, seemingly transparent in its lightness. All the sprawling activity from the last few days distilled into a glowing ember, it is as if Bhuwana Agung has returned to Bhuwana Alit.

The ceremony is now complete and, we all return to our homes."

"The next morning all that is left is the ritual debris; pieces of bamboo, palm leaves, little bags of plastic. The next time the calendar indicates it is time for this ceremony, the people will re-enact the entire process again. The essence is in the doing, this is a rehearsal for being Balinese. By means of the rituals in the temple the people remember how to arrange the elements from their own universes into a coherent form. It is how they find peace in a muddy river. The group becomes strong enough to pull in their members who have gone astray; teenagers without a clue, adults addicted to gambling or slipping into mental illness. Relationships descending into violence. All these can be redirected by the greater family of the temple. The culture becomes the template for a well-balanced life.

Even a leyak dream can be defeated. When the leyak approaches with hands ready to choke, the dreamer can simply say, "get away from me you old witch!"

And she will disappear."

more or less in line

Designs that contain
themselves – and
designs
that
need
borders

PART 06

NORTH BALI

The hills south of Tejakula village,
late afternoon.

Into the Arid, the North and East

There is a dramatic transition as you head northward between the slopes of Mount Agung and Mount Seraya. You travel through the thick forests and fertile ricefields of the south east, into the dusty plains and dry grasses of the North East coast. What happened to all the water? Considering that the rains of the rainy season usually blow from the north, one could imagine that this part of Bali would be the most wet and verdant.

The patterns made by the rains and the winds are complex and variable, so there is no easy answer to Bali's climatic puzzle. Perhaps the easiest way to understand north Bali's climate is by looking at the location of the mountains. The ridge of volcanic mountains that bisects Bali east to west are located much closer to the northern coast, and their slopes are much steeper than the slopes of the southern coast. When it does rain, very little of the water is absorbed into the ground, it tends to run off the slopes and back to the sea. So when the rains do arrive they are often in the form of flash floods, destructive and unpredictable. The arrival of the rains in the north is not the blessing of a nurturing, agricultural gift, as in the south. The hope for sustainable rain fall in the north often becomes the cause of fear and unease.

The driest area in Bali is the stretch between Tulamben and Kubu. At the height of the dry season, this area gives the impression of being uninhabitable, almost devoid of life. But an additional incident has bedeviled this specific area, the massive eruption of Mount Agung in 1963. The lava and poisonous gases ejected by this eruption caused island-wide destruction and suffering, and devastated the island's ecosystem. The area between Tulamben and Kubu in particular was hit hard and has yet to recover. It remains a very difficult place to live in.

During the sparse rainy season the landscape does get a dusting of green vegetation. And even during the dry season some plants can grow here; wild grasses, *kapok* trees, and cactus, whose bright red flowers enliven the sun burnt colors of the landscape. There is one tree that thrives in these dry areas—the *lontar* palm and it is the salvation of more than one arid tropical island. The local people have learned to use all the parts from bottom to top for their various daily needs. When found in its natural state, this tree has a full head of leaves. But when located near human settlements, most of the leaves get cut off and all that is left is a rather pitiful silhouette.

Lontar palms are helpful in another way. Their inflorescence produces a yeasty and frothy liquid that is slightly alcoholic, about as strong as beer. A glass of this liquid called "tuak" consumed in the hazy afternoons has helped many of the local inhabitants forget their daily challenges. If *tuak* is not strong enough, it can be distilled into a stronger drink called "arak" which can be as strong as the legendary (and rare) 80° proof variety. It doesn't take much *arak* to render the dry formidable environment tolerable and *Arak* is regularly sold from *warungs*. When *arak* producers bring their latest batch to a *warung*, the proprietor will then pour a small sample onto the wooden table to see if it burns, with its pretty blue flame. Because this "stress-reliever" is easily found and relatively inexpensive (even though it is technically illegal) unfortunately, there is widespread alcohol abuse with this drink. There is also the threat that a dishonest producer might spike the *arak* with methanol or paint solvent to give it that extra kick and sadly this drink has been known to kill.

Beach close to the Pura Segara, Tejakula village, North Bali.

Life on the Beach

"Houses with tin roofs are scattered around, grape vines hung over trellises offer some shade, a huge tree marks the village centre.

A quiet warung and a darkened room of men drinking and listening to someone singing about heroic deeds in an archaic language.

Nets on the beach are hanging to dry, the cock fight arena has been swept clean, rows of fishing boats in various states of disrepair.

The midday beach is populated only by a group of noisy boys and salt makers tending their vats of sea water quickly evaporating and leaving glistening salt crystals behind. A light breeze blows steadily. A local man climbs a coconut tree to harvest some of the fruit. He chops them off with a cleaver, and proudly shows the scar on his hand from his latest cleaver accident. He is short and built like a boxer, his wife is stout and robust. She gets some cucumbers from the garden and four smoked flying fish from the neighbor. It all adds up to a fine meal to watch the colours of the ocean, metallic shades of blue, green, and silver, the setting sun adds unlikely tones of yellow and orange."

Turning to the Sea

Another strategy to survive this arid environment is to turn away from the hills and look to the sea. Generally speaking the Balinese don't like the ocean, but know when to put it to good use. In the arid regions the people turn to the land to grow peanuts, fruit, and vegetables, and when it dries up they turn to the sea.

The Balinese react instinctively with fear to the ocean; they might never see beauty in the mysteries of the deep water. Even so, they have a long relationship with the waters that surround them. Their boats are very fish-like, something like half fish, half boat. The bow is in the shape of a fish with open mouth and bulging eyes. When the fishermen go out at night their lamps are seen as dots of light in the darkness, floating resolutely on the surface of the black ocean.

Stingray
Tropical Grouper
Surgeonfish
Bicolor Doty Back
Octopus

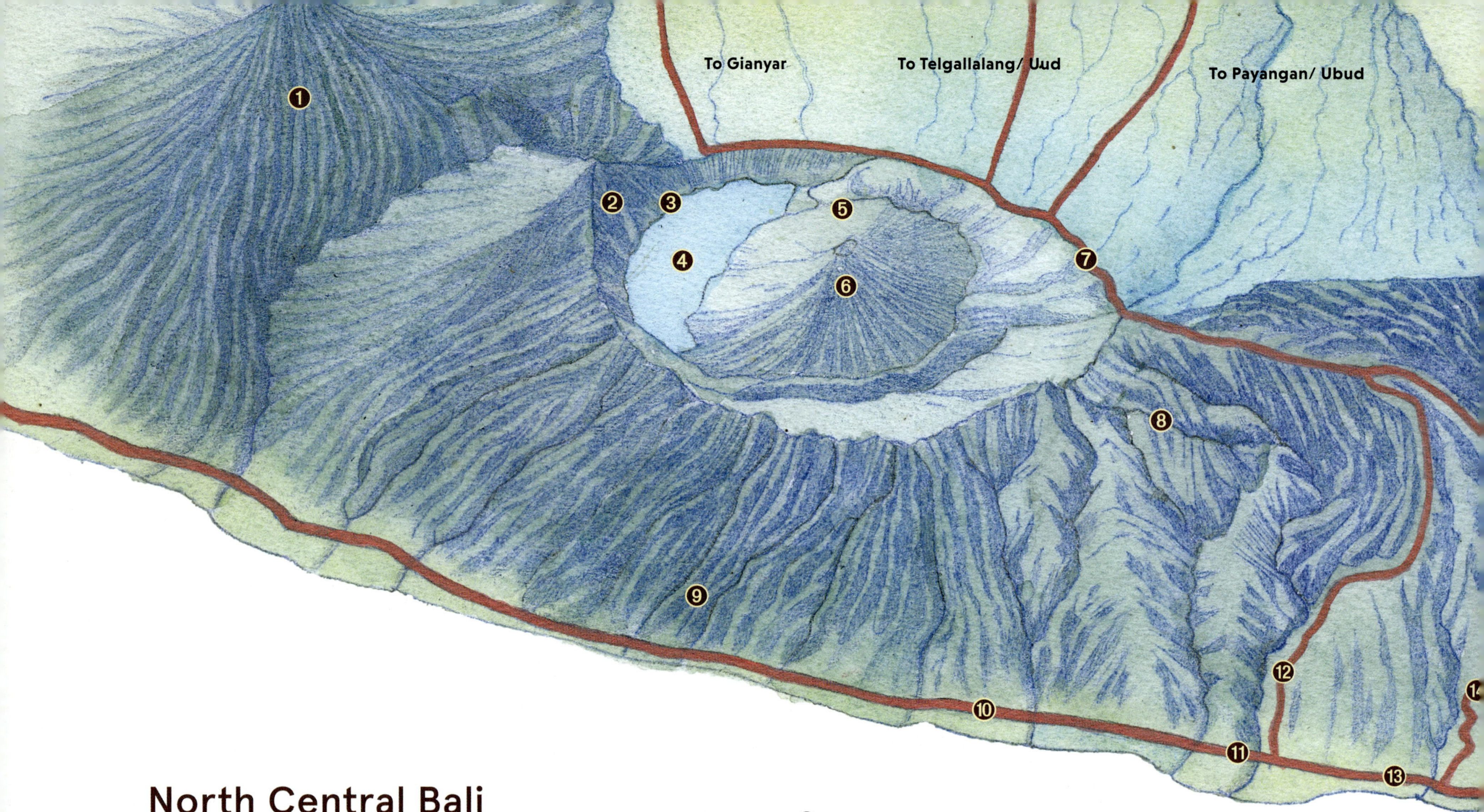

North Central Bali

The Regency of North Bali is called "Buleleng" and it offers the visitor another variation on the Balinese character and way of life. The people from the north are known for being down to earth and straight to the point. They speak the least refined form of the Balinese language with little regard for hierarchical manoeuvering. Their *gamelans* play an aggressive, muscular beat, and their dancers sometimes dance so fiercely that sweat drips off the tips of their noses as they perform.

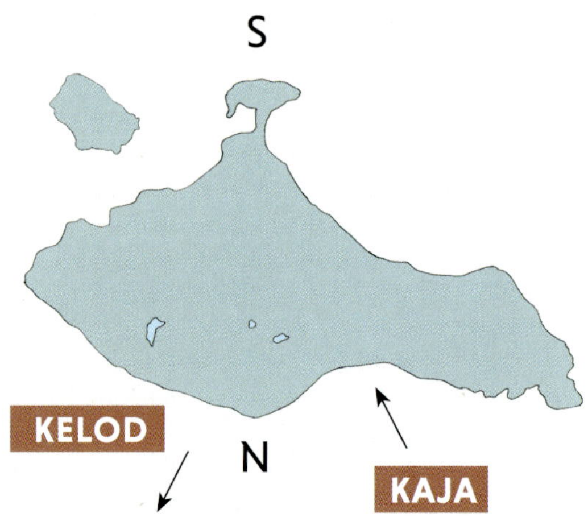

According to the norms of cartography, this map is upside down. But this is the way North Balinese people see their island. Notice that *Kaja* and *Kelod* also are inverted compared to the South Bali orientation, but they retain their orienting function, *Kaja* to the mountain and *Kelod* to the sea.

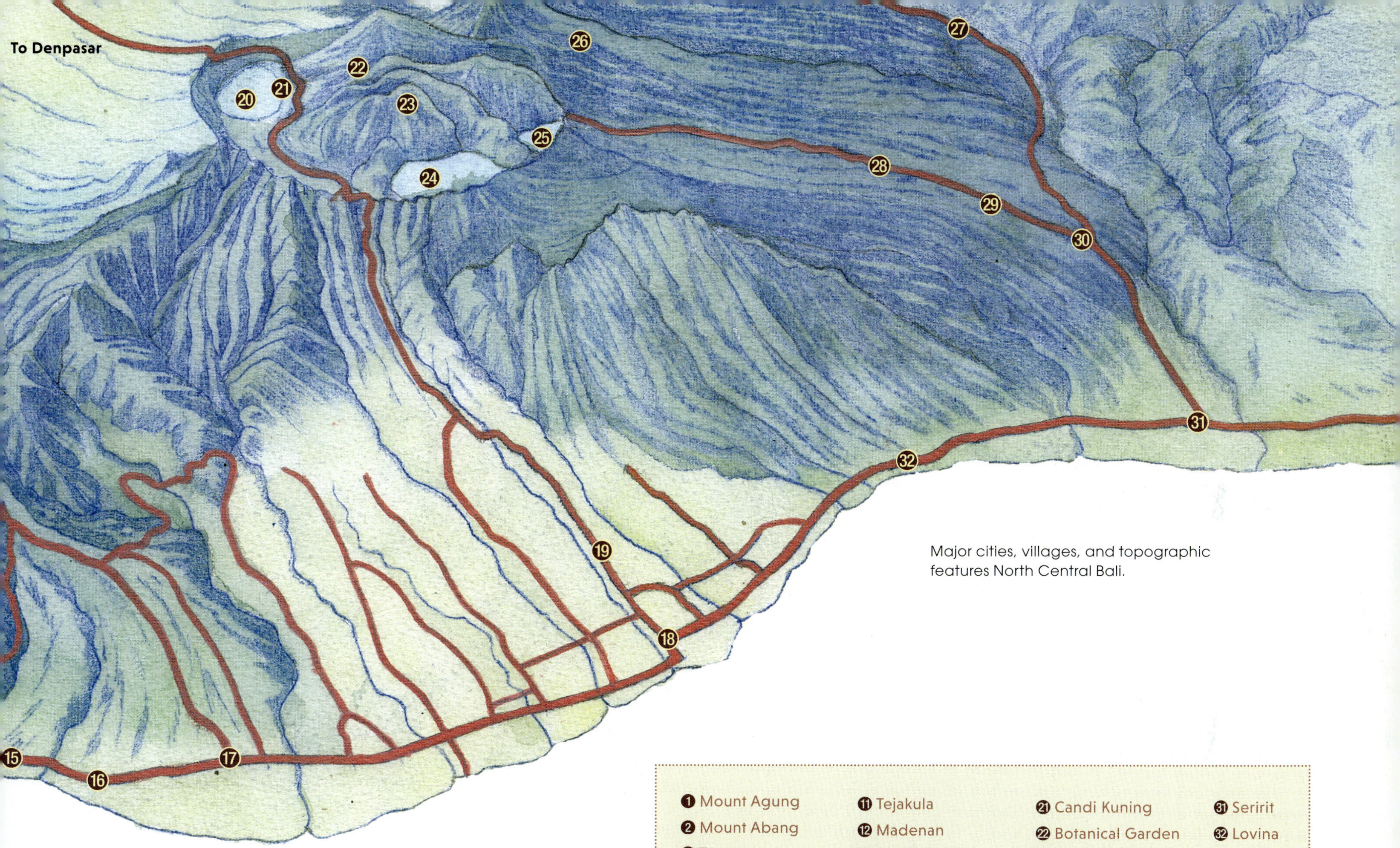

Major cities, villages, and topographic features North Central Bali.

1. Mount Agung
2. Mount Abang
3. Terunyan
4. Lake Batur
5. Toya Bungkah
6. Mount Batur
7. Kintamani
8. Sukawana
9. Tianyar
10. Sambirenteng
11. Tejakula
12. Madenan
13. Bondalam
14. Sembiran
15. Julah
16. Pacung
17. Kubutambahan
18. Singaraja
19. Gitgit
20. Lake Bratan
21. Candi Kuning
22. Botanical Garden
23. Mount Tapak
24. Lake Buyan
25. Lake Tamblingan
26. Mount Batukaru
27. Pupuan
28. Munduk
29. Banyuatis
30. Mayong
31. Seririt
32. Lovina

The boat illustrated is a fishing boat from East Java, anchored at a harbour close to Perancak Village, Negara.

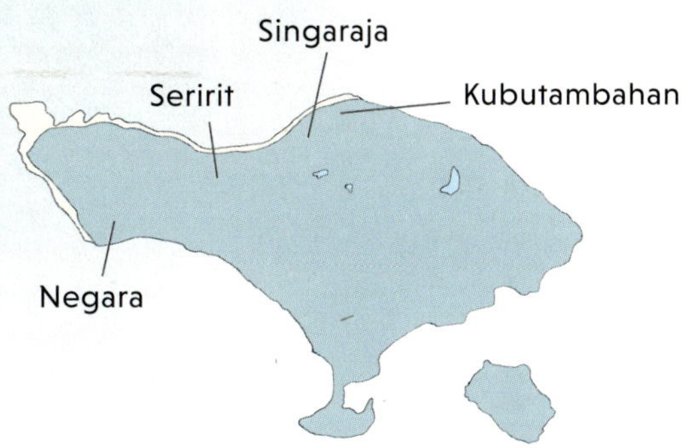

Pesisir Culture

The line of volcanic mountains that bisects Bali east to west doesn't run through the centre of the island, but lies much closer to the northern coast. In some north coast locations it seems the mountains run directly to the ocean. This means that North Bali doesn't have the long and gentle plains and terraced rice fields that are found in the south; there is no rice bowl here.

You will find a coastal road running along the narrow lip of flat land between the mountains and the ocean; this road runs the entire coast from east to west. Strung along this road are a series of villages that seem remote, but at an earlier time were relatively cosmopolitan. This is because the north coast is where the world first visited Bali; waters are calmer here and harbours easier to establish. In fact, the oldest known architectural finds in Bali were found on the present day village of Julah, about 20 km east of Singaraja. This village was also the first place mentioned in the historical record. There are references to anchorages found near this village.

As history unfolded, the trading routes within the Indonesian Archipelago were established along the northern coast. These routes were travelled mainly by Javanese traders but other traders used the same pathways—especially the most famous Indonesian seafarers, the Bugis. Along with these local traders came the Chinese, Arabs, and eventually the Europeans. All these groups made their stamp on the life on these coastal settlements, leaving behind merchants and agents, priests and monks. A syncretic culture evolved in the larger of these trader towns which is called "Pesisir", loosely translated as the 'culture of the coast'. Pesisir culture is the hallmark of many coastal communities in Indonesia. In Bali the cities that could claim to be pesisir are Singaraja, Seririt, and Negara, with Singaraja being the most intact of the three.

Singaraja

The major city in the north is Singaraja. In fact, until the middle of the 20th Century it was the only major point of entry to Bali. During this time, from the mid-19th Century until around 1939, Singaraja was a flourishing place with separate quarters for the Europeans, Bugis, Chinese and Arab inhabitants. Singaraja had temples (both Hindu and Confucian), mosques and churches. All of these elements of the city are still intact and active today.

After the Indonesian Independence in 1945, the political centre of Bali was moved from Singaraja to Denpasar. Then the international airport was built close to Kuta in 1967, and the world's attention to Bali was firmly grounded in the south, leaving Singaraja somewhat disengaged.

It still remains the urban centre for the north and is a magnet for the northern villages, with its universities, hospitals, and employment opportunities. But compared with the newly internationalized south, Singaraja feels cut off and arrested. However, seemingly oblivious to other people's perceptions, it maintains its singular identity, and continues on as it has in the past, moving at its own speed.

Given Singaraja's identity as a Pesasir city, there are a number of different architectural styles represented there. The first (seen above) is the former palace of the royal family of Buleleng. It shows a clear Dutch influence; this synthesis is known as the "Dutch Indies style". The same influence is seen in this private residence, below.

To the left is the oldest Mosque in Signaraja, Masjid Nur. It is a good example of Islamic architectural design often found in the older mosques of Java.

"It is hot during midday, the sunlight is like a physical force. It chases the people into dark interior spaces and creates a strange emptiness on the streets.

At 4 pm a single cloud floats over the city, drops its rain and then disappears. The music of the shadow puppet play, the wayang gender, is broadcast through loudspeakers. The music hovers over the traffic after the rain. The lamp of the minaret of Nur Mosque glows green against the afternoon sky, legions of birds forming and unforming around it.

In the early evening when it cools down, the store lights blaze and illuminate their brightly coloured doors and walls, revealing the brightest colours this town can offer. People wander the sidewalks looking at the merchandise and listen to the pop music spilling onto the streets. At the bus terminal a conductor, with a face ravaged by chicken pox scars, is at ease after a long day. He plays chess with his associates. Punishment for losing is to play the next round with a dead battery tied around one's ear.

Later, past midnight, a group of men returning from a temple ceremony stop at a warung in the main market for a snack. They are hosted by the woman running the warung and her three weary daughters. An angry man confronts a wandering dog who jumped on a pile of goods to bark at him. A cat watches lazily as an enormous rat saunters past. People guarding their goods are wrapped in sarongs and sleeping on their boxes. The temple festival was not far away and still in full swing. Someone reaches over and turns off the radio in the warung so they can listen to the ancient music from the temple—klang klang klang klang klang, together with incantations from a male chorus and a pack of dogs howling in the distance."

One Road.
Tejakula-Lateng

There aren't many roads going from the coast to the mountains; the topography doesn't encourage road building. The roads that do exist in this area tend to wind and turn along the ridges of hills. Only if necessary do they make acrobatic dives in and out of valleys.

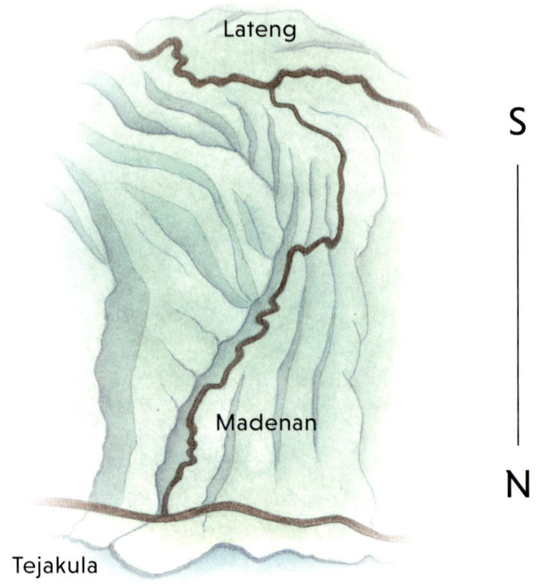

The two texts to the right are glimpses of a well known road from the village of Lateng, passing through the village of Madenan, and arriving at the coastal village of Tejkula. This road is for experienced and attentive drivers only.

5:00 AM, Up the Hill

"A slight glow in the eastern sky, the stars beginning to fade. Some clouds catch the first light from the hidden sun. Further up, the sky turns overcast until it is thick with fog and strong winds blow the trees wildly.

A single bird flies directly in front, leading the way along the broken line in the middle of the road. Suddenly, the fog lifts and shows that the dawn has arrived quietly, delirious greens and gold and the ocean is a shimmering blue."

6:45 PM, Down the Hill

"A slight glow in the western sky, a crescent moon with two or three stars. The parched ground glows deep red and gives back heat to the sky. Passing through a village, a gamelan is rehearsing and a dancer is working out in a patch of fluorescent light.

Further down the road, a burning coconut tree drops sparks on the ground. In the distance, the ocean is slightly mottled in the dimness, a cluster of tiny lights from the fishing boats headed out to sea."

The villages that have grown along these mountain roads are isolated and idiosyncratic with unique identities and ways of living. You can spot unusual things in these hidden places.

This motorcycle was found unattended on a mountain road close to Catur village. It clearly is a working bike, but still is in beautiful condition. Everything seems to be original, from the olive green paint to the leather covered foot petals.

Kebun Culture

When travelling through the hillsides, both north and south, it will become quickly clear that you are not in rice country any more. These villages owe their livelihoods to the fruit trees and coffee bushes that thrive at these altitudes. There is a wide variety of cultivated plants in these areas. Within a relatively small space you can find vanilla, chocolate, durian, cloves, cashews, and coffee all mixed together. Like a bistro whose menu has lost its focus!

The word 'kebun' is difficult to translate. The closest word is "plantation", but this conjures up images of tidy rows of cultivated plants; this is not usually the case with Balinese kebun. There are some areas of cultivation with a semblance of order, but the majority of these orchards appear wonderfully chaotic. It would be easy for you to pass by and not even know that agriculture was being practised here. It takes a while to focus on the logic of it all, which simply amounts to planting small things under tall things, the larger trees providing shelter to the smaller and more sensitive plants.

And in the end there is wisdom in this jumble of plants. No single tree is allowed to dominate, the plants are more resistant to disease and climatic changes. In short, the whole enterprise is highly sustainable.

The two plants most often found in kebun are clove and coffee.

Working drawing, coffee tree, North Bali.

Cloves

Myrtaceae Syzygium aromaticum

Some historical texts credit the Dutch with the 'discovery' of this plant. Indeed, before World War Two, the Dutch and the clove tree were still firmly identified together in the western imagination. However, the 'discovery' of this plant far predates the Dutch presence in South East Asia, and forms a long list of varied interests throughout history. The first known trade in cloves was done by the Chinese in the First Century AD, then there was involvement by Arab merchants based in Mallaca. Next, the Portugese appeared briefly, followed by the Spanish and English. Eventually, the Dutch returned to dominance and monopolized the trade in cloves at the end of the 17th Century. After some time, they were not able to maintain this monopoly and the cultivation and distribution was shared with the French, British, East Africans, and Indians. Together with nutmeg, cloves actually played an historically important role in the international balance of power during the colonial era.

Clove is a lovely tree, a member of the Myrtaceae family, which also includes the lofty eucalyptus. It has a loosely conical shape and delicate colouring which ranges from deep olive to a yellowish peach color in the young leaves. But it is the aroma of the oil produced by the flowers which gives this plant such a legendary history.

The Chinese considered the clove blossoms to be an aphrodisiac, and that is easy to understand. Perhaps you will be fortunate enough to travel through mountain villages during the clove harvest. The flowers are spread out on mats to dry in the clear sunlight and cool mountain air. The sweet and complex aroma infuses the surroundings and creates a large scale aromatherapy session, a truly democratic gift from nature.

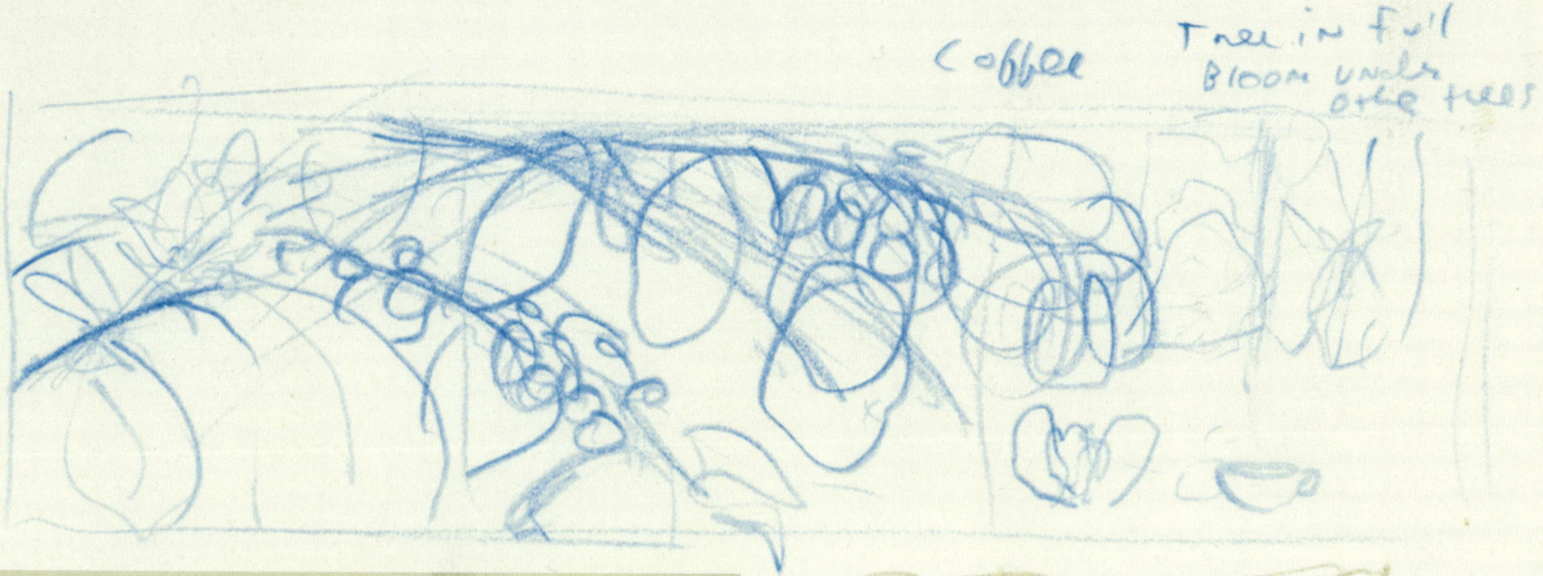

Drawing from a coffee plantation, Munduk village, North Bali.

Coffee

Rubiaceae Coffea

The flowers appear at the beginning of the rainy season. There are three or four buds in each flower cluster, and each tree can produce thousands of flowers. A tree in full bloom looks like it is dusted with snow, and fills the surrounding area with a delicate aroma.

The harvesting and preparation of the beans is labour- intensive and requires patience. But the roasting process requires skill and experience, and is the key to quality coffee. Roasting the beans at the wrong temperature, or for the wrong period of time, can mean the difference between coffee that is full and rich, or flat and bitter.

Coffee Growth Stages

Balian River, South Western Bali.

The West, the Border of Cultivation

The north western coast is a quiet place; except for one road and some scattered villages this is uncultivated land. This area is a protected forest called the "West Bali National Park". This forest has been left undeveloped, although there are persistent of illegal logging here.

There is a stark contrast between the cultivated and uncultivated areas, as can be seen in the aerial view to the left. On the southwestern part of Bali, the Balian River separates the east from the west. The eastern side is fully cultivated and the western side has been more or less left alone. The Balian River marks this transition; it looks like two different islands have been stuck together at this point.

It is not easy to get into the National Park. If you are found there by a government official you will be asked to show your entrance permit. This area is most easily seen by driving around the perimeter and looking into the dense vegetation. There are massive trees emerging from the mass of smaller ones showing every conceivable shade of green. This is an area that seems to be undeveloped, but it is better to say that it has 'self-developed' and grown according to its own logic of interconnected systems of balance and exchange. It would require a book itself to unravel the complexity of this eco system, so for the purposes of this project it will be left as a mystery, seen only as a glimpse from the outside.

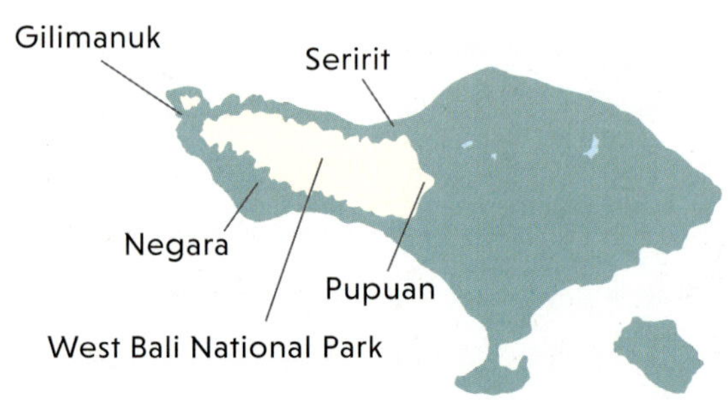

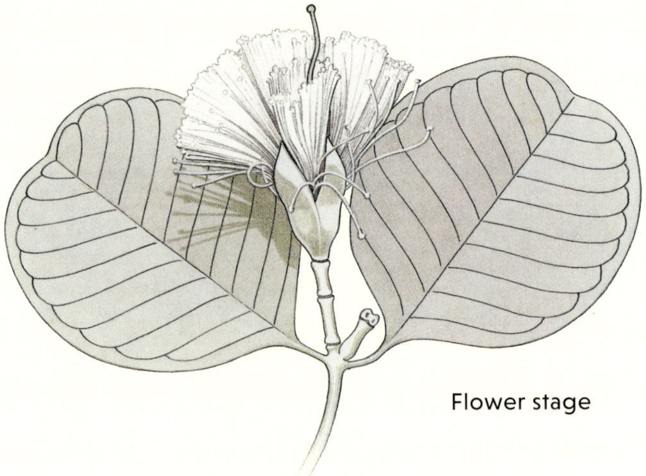

Flower stage

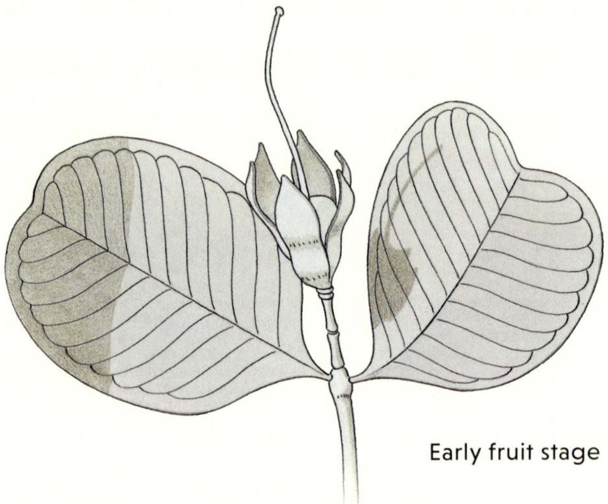

Early fruit stage

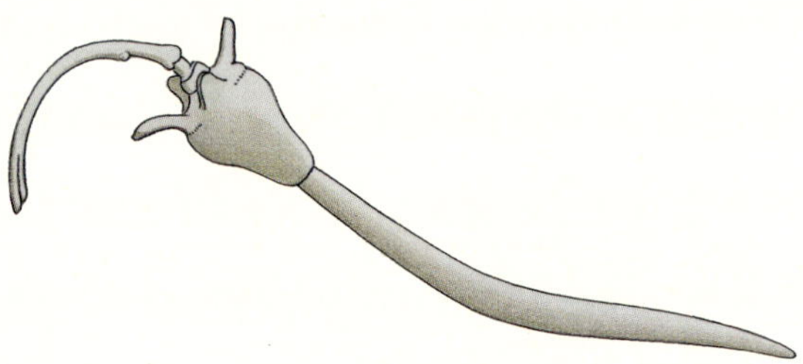

Late fruit stage

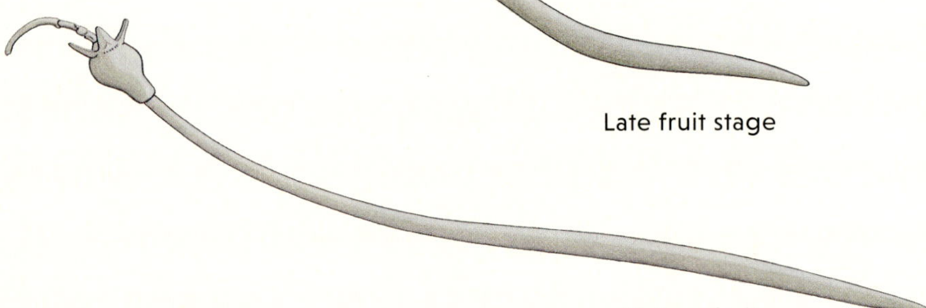

Mature fruit

Mangrove Swamps

There is one element of the forest ecosystem that is very accessible, but until recently hardly noticed. These are the humble mangrove swamps.

Mangrove trees are not very pretty and grow in ill-smelling places, so they can be easily passed by in favour of more 'aesthetic' trees. But ecologists see these trees as primadonnas due to their ability to grow right at the shoreline, where both fresh and salt water mix. By growing exactly at this area, the colonies of mangrove trees help stabilize the shoreline, which helps to reduce erosion and also provides a habitat for a variety of species. They also have beautiful flowers which, when fertilized, grow into long torpedo-shaped fruit. This fruit actually begins to germinate and grow roots while still connected to the tree. Eventually, it drops into the mud where it either joins the pile of other dried-up seed pods, or takes hold in the mud and begins life as a new tree.

These mangrove seedlings grow obediently in straight rows at a mangrove research centre south of Negara, in western Bali. Even at this early stage in their development, their root architecture is easily visible. As these trees mature, these roots will develop into a thick tangle of arching roots, like a tangle of limbs. Some trees look like they could stand up and just walk away.

Scene from the Botanical Garden. The towering trees create cool, shady places to relax.

Conservation Kebun Raya

As noted earlier, it is not easy to gain access to the forests of western Bali. This area is intended to be a sanctuary for Balinese flora and fauna. There is another option, however, for a person who wants to get a taste of nature, or an afternoon jaunt with the family in the woods. There is a user-friendly forest near Lake Bratan that is more than happy to receive visitors. It is called “Kebun Raya” and is Bali’s botanical garden. Established in 1959, it is located about one hour north of Denpasar and is a local favourite for a family picnic on the weekend.

It is not an internationally renowned botanical garden, but it has developed infrastructure in recent years to explain the workings of a forest to the residents and visitors to Bali. There are orchid and cactus gardens, and an area devoted to medicinal plants. There are signs identifying the unusual trees and where they originate.

But it is the park grounds themselves that make this a special place. There are tall shady trees filling this area and spacious grass-covered ground where the sun filters through. On weekends, it is especially busy. Families relax together after the mad dash up from Denpasar, with lots of kids running around, and music from radios. A general bustle, just like a popular park should be.

But there are quiet corners at the fringes of this property where the air is crisp and the wind blows through the stately trees. This is a favourite destination for young lovers. More than one romance has taken root in the hidden areas of this park.

A pair of Bali Starlings, Payangan village.

This lovely bird is found only in the wild areas of north western Bali, and is exceedingly rare. It has been long feared in danger of becoming extinct. Fortunately, through the help of conservationists, it is making a comeback in captivity and has become emblematic of efforts to protect Bali's ecosystem.

PART 07

URBAN BALI

Introduction to Urban Bali, 3 sites

On the road heading east out of the airport there are three sites located directly on the airport's boundary that unintentionally provide three vivid clues to life in urban Bali.

The first site is located on a small plot of land on the northwest corner of the intersection between Jalan Bandera and Jalan Tuban. This small parcel of land contains three buildings: a Hindu temple; an Islamic mosque; and a Christian church. These three houses of worship are basically located at the same address. They are so crowded together that they most likely share electrical and plumbing facilities; they at least have a common parking area. In Indonesia it is not uncommon to see houses of worship from various faiths located side by side in a peaceful coexistence, a sight that would be unthinkable in many countries. The Indonesians are justifiably proud of their religious tolerance. These three buildings are also a reminder that Indonesia is a religious society, the belief that God does not exist is incomprehensible to the vast majority of Indonesians. Many public gatherings are begun and ended with an ecumenical prayer. This is also true of the public schools as well as with many private parties.

The second site is a white concrete statue located across the street from the temple, mosque and church. This imposing, larger than life, statue depicts Gatot Kaca sacrificing himself to Karna in the climactic battle of the Mahabhrata, one of the bedrocks of Asian mythology. This statue is a favourite gathering place for local people, especially when it is illuminated by spotlights in the cool of the evening.

Gatot Kaca is shown in his full glory pointing his finger arrogantly at his opponent. He is a fine figure of a man, but this hero is totally imaginary and has never walked the face of the earth. This statue is a reminder that myths conceived

in the distant past still have a powerful hold over the popular imagination. There is a deep feeling in Bali for mythic worlds, and there is a powerful attraction to the stories and lessons of mythology.

The third sight is located further down the road; it is a life-sized statue of Lieutenant Colonel I Gusti Ngurah Rai, a modern mythic figure for the Balinese. He is seen in a casual, almost matter-of-fact, pose, portrayed as a very real mortal man (in contrast to the glamour and theatrics of Gatot Kaca). Ngurah Rai was a guerilla fighter in Indonesia's war for independence from the Dutch after the Second World War. Together with his small band of fighters, they fought to the death to secure the sovereignty of his island and nation. His statue is an unassuming, but nevertheless stark, reminder of the price paid by an earlier generation of Indonesians in winning their independence within living memory.

An Island within an Island

There is a heavily developed area in the southern tip of the island. It is densely populated and has an enormous economic importance for all the people living in Bali. Urban Bali is a dense, sprawling, visually saturated environment of businesses and residences. Some visitors to the island spend their time here exclusively, whether in holidays of several days, or establishing themselves here for many years. This is an insulated, self-contained place capable of providing a full and satisfying life to its residents. Very clearly, an island within an island.

Even though some Balinese consider urban Bali home, it was largely built due to the efforts of other people, Indonesians from other islands, and visitors from around the world. This remains a place where many Balinese feel like outsiders, a place to make some money and establish careers, and then return to more familiar places. The majority of these Balinese migrant workers will insulate themselves from this alien world and return home relatively unchanged. Others will attempt to engage the foreign community on a deeper level and form relationships within its social parameters. And an extremely small minority will embrace internationalism fully and reject their own culture altogether. But while each person is charting their own course, they at least have the opportunity to witness the carnival of international life, amusing and sometimes inexplicable, that has arrived at their shores.

Urban Bali is a study in itself with its own rhythm and nuance, but for this brief look will be divided into three sections: Nusa Dua, Kuta, and Denpasar.

Nusa Dua

This is where the Indonesians first learned to implement the concept of paradise onto Bali; it is a place where everything becomes well-considered and coherent. Nusa Dua was first planned in the 1970s as an enclave of five-star hotels located at the southern tip of the island that had been declared under- utilized. It was a very self-conscious attempt to create an image of what the outside world thought Bali should look like. The entire landscape is micro-managed, every detail has been considered. Water is pumped in, wastes are pumped out. Truckloads of dancers and musicians in full regalia arrive each night to perform; nocturnal gardens are illuminated from strange angles, seemingly creating new hybrid species of botanica.

And it all works very well. Nusa Dua is host to many of Bali's visitors and is also the site for major international conventions and governmental meetings. The image of Bali as a hotel in paradise has been firmly implanted in the global imagination; the standard reference to Bali by news organizations around the world is 'the resort island'. Many visitors go no farther than the confines of this area, enjoying the fabrication of the place, and are well-satisfied with their trip. Who wouldn't want to be a modern day Adam or Eve strolling around in the garden- especially after all the serpents had been carefully removed?

Spa Culture

Begining in the 1990s the concept of paradise has been taken to the limits of its expression. This phase of the paradise industry has been the series of spas that have sprung up all over urban Bali. The degree of sophistication a spa displays and the benefits promised to the customer depend on the price. The more modest spas have lush, luxurious environments and promise a relaxing visit. But as a spa becomes more exclusive, the lushness makes way for cleaner lines and more expansive spaces. Visitors are picked up in private cars and are whisked away to discrete locations with minimalistic interiors. Here, the concept of relaxation evolves into the concept of wellness and eventually flirts with the concept of spirituality. It is no surprise that the subsequent stage of spa culture was the blossom of wedding chapels appearing throughout the island.

Kuta Beach

In contrast to the intentionality of Nusa Dua, Kuta looks like a place that just happened by itself. It is the most cosmopolitan spot in Bali and has the best people-watching in the entire Indonesian Archipelago. It is the first spot where foreign-controlled commerce began and it remains intensely commercial. Even books about Kuta are full of advertisements. It runs 24 hours a day transforming itself hour by hour into different spot for different people. At 5 AM it is a typical Indonesian city with its traditional markets in full swing, local people buying and selling the goods necessary for their everyday lives. Beginning at mid-morning it becomes a shopping extravaganza, offering the gamut from sweaty and frenetic family-run art shops to hushed, air conditioned, high-end retail. While the sun shines the beach is in its glory. You can see Islamic women, covered with long flowing robes that allow none of their skin to show, next to other women who are wearing bikinis and are almost naked. In the evening Kuta offers up the spectrum of world cuisine, from local foods served in plastic bowls, to elegant dining where savoury morsels are artfully placed on oversized ceramics. Later in the evening the air is full of rhythms - Techno, Reggae, R&B - while party-goers roam through the nightclub districts. When the bars close down at 3 AM, the street life gets a little strange until the last of the night shift has finally retired. Soon afterwards the market folk head out again with yawns and sleepy eyes to start the whole cycle over again.

People come to Kuta for many reasons: to relax, to have fun, to work. The differing interests and approaches to life by these various groups of people make this a fragmented place. It's not so much a community as an interface of distinct and sometimes contradictory interests jostling for predominance. But for the Balinese Hindus who were born here, there is another layer of meaning in Kuta that is not a readily apparent to the casual observer. Whereas outsiders might divide up this area into different types of entertainment or shopping districts, the native Balinese Hindus define this area according to the three main village temples. These temples are the traditional ceremonial centres for Kuta's native Hindus, even though the visual prominence of these temples is somewhat obscured by modern development.

Despite their low profile they continue to define life in Kuta for their members. The traditional social system they represent overshadows all the glittering growth in Kuta during the last 40 years. When it is time for a religious procession to leave one of these three temples and march along the congested main street of Kuta, the rest of life is required to pause for a moment. The Balinese who are conducting the ceremony are very polite about it, and efficient in organizing the activity with their walkie-talkies and cell phones. But it is clearly understood that everyone else will wait for the ceremony to proceed. This hierarchy is never questioned or violated.

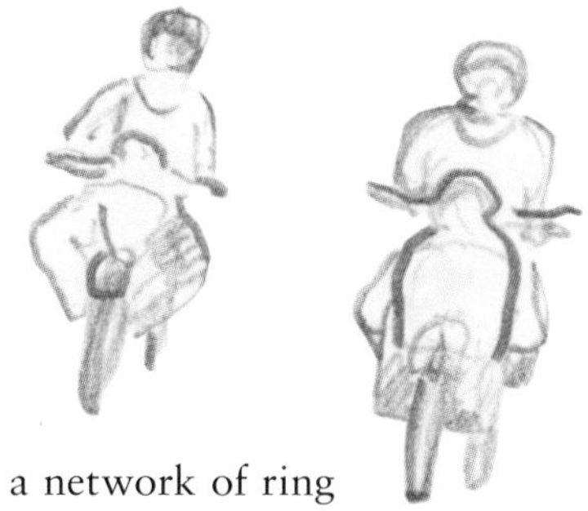

Ring Road Culture

As urban Bali has expanded rapidly during the last 30 years, the local government has constructed a network of ring roads to reduce traffic congestion. The entire urban area is bounded and bisected by this series of expressways. As they frame and divide the urban area, they cut into earlier road systems leaving bizarrely shaped bits of roads and fragments of neighbourhoods behind. These super roads have been imposed on the landscape by committee decision; they don't feel organic and they have a clear industrial quality to them.

But at the major intersections of these ring roads there has grown up a specific sub-culture with its own identity. Groups of men and boys, each with something to sell, establish their own territories here and vie for the attention of the drivers waiting for the lights to change. There are skinny boys in baggy pants selling newspapers (both local and international), sometimes a crippled man is playing a harmonica for tips, another man is selling wind-up helicopters, sailing up and over the vehicles. Another day a man is sitting forlornly next to a rack of blonde wigs, feeling dejected because nobody is buying his wares. The drivers show interest if they want, but when the light changes from red to green these crossroad entrepreneurs had better get out of the way. The race is on again to see which of the drivers will win the right of way this time around.

There is nothing too certain in the jumble of vehicles, it's not as much a matter of traffic rules as traffic scenarios, the right of way belongs to whoever gets there first, the rules of the road are being constantly re-written. Some drivers are tense, some are spaced-out, any one driver might change between these moods during the course of a short journey. But since these big roads are crowded and hot, with much blue exhaust lingering in the air, you should not expect to find many easy-going drivers here. It's tough to be a cool driver on a hot road.

There are trucks and buses here, too many of them like whales flopping in a puddle. There are quite a few private sedans and mini vans, with the windows tightly closed, the passengers trying to maintain the illusion that they are in climate controlled, mobile lounges. Any remaining space is filled with motorcycles, thousands of them. The truck drivers call them "mosquitoes", swarming around and becoming a nuisance. The 2 wheelers use their manoeuverability almost like a weapon as they twist and turn and dart around, spitting out blue smoke.

The larger vehicles more or less drive wherever they want, with an air of inevitability generated by their large mass. Their drivers sit high above the mayhem, unaffected and imperturbable. Not so the motor cycle drivers; down in the thick of the noise and smoke they are the wild cards, they have the potential of making incredibly unlikely and dangerous moves. It almost seems that a number of these death wish drivers actually want to get hit. The perception changes somewhat if you became a motorcycle driver yourself. You will get the glimmer of the notion that there is always enough room for at least one more motorcycle to squeeze in, just enough space to pass by and not get hit. There is an almost irresistible urge to maintain a forward motion in spite of the obvious hazards.

If you are driving when the schools get out, the craziness goes up a notch or two. Hormone-fired teenagers spill out into the street, oblivious to the machines of steel and rubber trying their best to avoid them. The boy drivers talk the loudest and make the biggest show of themselves, contorting into strange positions as they drive. They sometime punch holes into their mufflers to turn them into amplifiers, assuming the girls will like them better for it. But most girls drive with perfect posture, crisp, cool, and unaffected by all the confusion around them, except for an occasional highly-refined look of annoyance when they have to drive through someone's cloud of smoke.

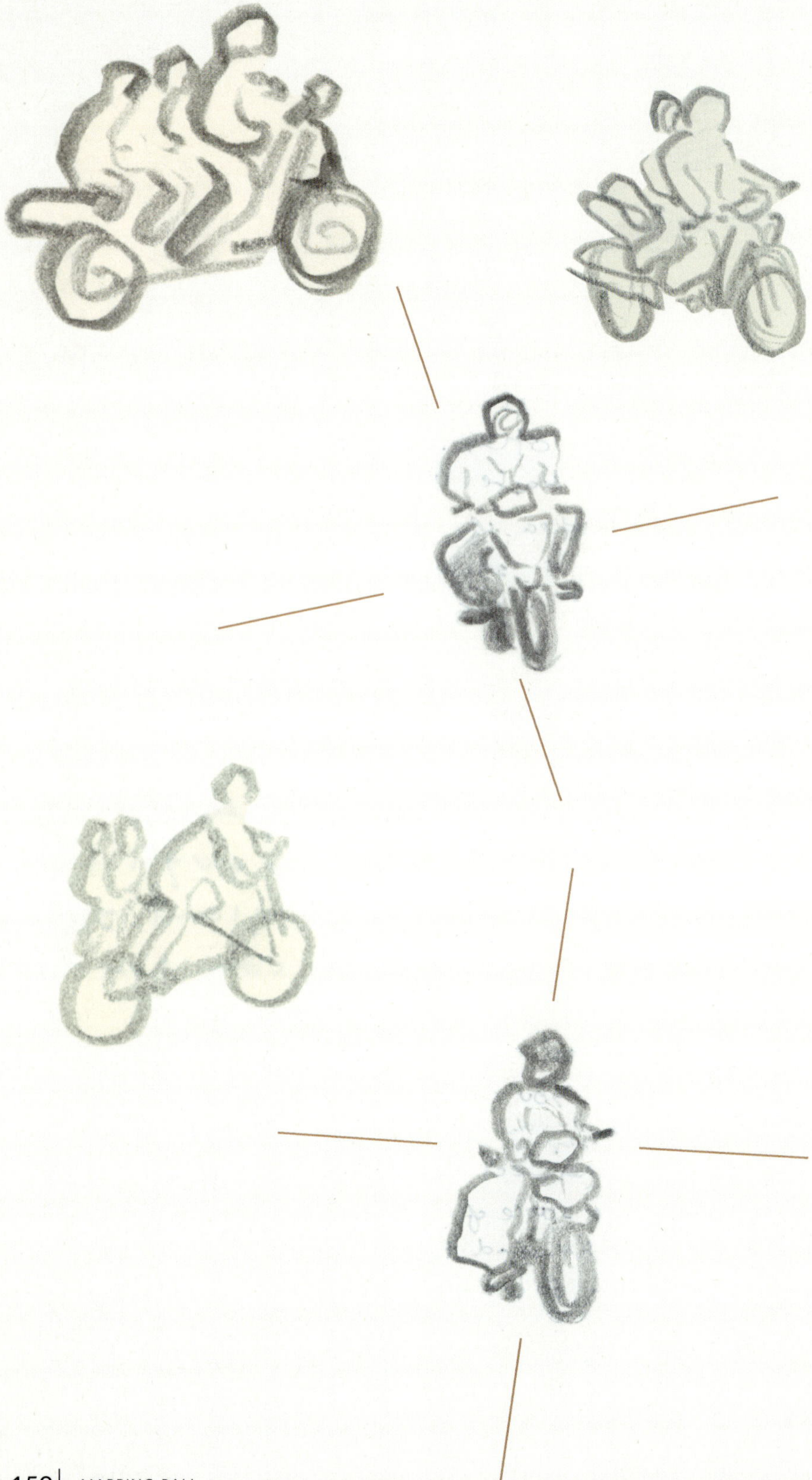

The Metaphysics of Driving?

Our minds crave coherence, and we try to make sense of this theatre of chaos. If none can be found we might turn to metaphysical answers. Do the Balinese believe that the roads are an interface between life and death, an arena where the forces of fate ultimately determine who falls and who doesn't? Do they believe that these incidents on the road have all been predetermined and are largely beyond an individual's control? Why else would a mother hold her baby in one arm and drive with the other? Or why would a young man drive through rush hour traffic one-handed while sending a text message on his cell phone?

A young person's first major motorcycle accident is something like a modern rite of passage; it provides a good story to tell and a moderate scar on the body for life. In some ways these experiences are seen as brushes with Fate. There are deeply felt beliefs among the Balinese that there are forces at work in their lives that are beyond an individual's control. But even for spiritually inclined people like the Balinese, it's hard to accept that they surrender themselves to Fate on the road. Much of the road behaviour in Bali is simply bad driving. The smiles and laughter after a near miss on the road (behaviour most Balinese people find very hard to explain) seems less laughing at Fate and more a nervous response to what nearly happened.

But sometimes it does happen. Usually it is just a damaged bike and a bloody knee. But other times you could pass the scene of an incident, scattered bits of plastic and glass on the road, with a spot of fresh blood nearby: probably a head injury. Somewhere a family is thrust into an abrupt and intense tragedy.

“At the warung of Ibu Putu, the news was told of Kadek’s death last night in a motorcycle accident; her two sisters told the story. It was at night, Kadek was riding on the back of her boyfriend’s cycle when he tried to pass a car on a blind curve. They hit another motorcycle head-on. Kadek died instantly, two other people are in bad shape. Her sister, her eyes blazing said, “You should have seen her, her brains were coming out her ears!” The other sister simply said, “It was fate.”

Back at the house a reception was underway. Her mother had been in shock since she heard the news, finally getting an injection from a doctor to help her face the mourners. One of the cousins passed around the photo album of Kadek’s body being ritually washed before her burial. Her family gathered around her naked, crushed body, one uncle holding his hand above her most intimate area to preserve some of her modesty as the camera intruded into the hushed gathering.

This was Kadek’s third motorcycle accident that happened on almost the same date in the month of August. Whether this was a coincidence or a cosmic sign, this pattern gave some peace to her family. There was apparently no anger directed to the young man who caused the accident.”

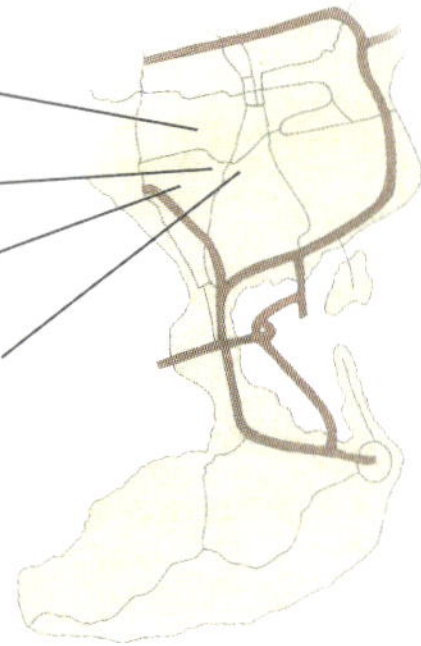

Denpasar, Old Urban

The area enclosed by the network of ring roads is called "Denpasar". It is Bali's largest city, hot and frenetic with an intense physicality that can be challenging to those of us more accustomed to the detachment of cyberspace. But if you are prepared for a sensory onslaught, you can discover in Denpasar an eclectic selection of goods from the entire Indonesian Archipelago. You will be able to find many layers from Bali's past and present history. Denpasar is one place in metro Bali where the Balinese don't feel like they are in someone else's city.

The downtown area was formally South Bali's commercial centre. It is now somewhat derailed by the massive retail complexes in the tourist areas, but it still chugs along with a whiff of nostalgia. The two most vibrant areas of downtown are the Kumbasari Market and the gold district.

"Kumbasari" is the name of the main market, which is actually a series of markets that hit their stride around 1 AM. While most of Denpasar sleeps, people from the villages throughout Bali bring in fresh produce to sell to the urban population. The market is understood to be a woman's world; there are men here but they play a clearly defined supporting role. The market is one of the few public place in Bali where the women tell the men where to go and what to do. It is also a fiercely competitive place where you can find a whole row of merchants side by side selling exactly the same thing, each one trying to capture the buyer's attention by talking louder than the others.

Close to the market is the gold district. The gold shops are always busy because the Balinese have an inexhaustible fascination with gold. It can be used as equity: gold is often purchased whenever a little extra money finds its way into a Balinese household and is seen as a sort of savings account. If the need for money quickly arises, this gold can be easily sold. The beauty of gold is that while in someone's possession it can be used as an adornment, especially at the time of a temple ceremony. It gives tangible evidence of a family's current economic position. Gold gives more pleasure to the owner than the abstract numbers listed in a bank statement. Buying and selling gold is a Balinese obsession and these gold shops are always doing a good business.

Also in this area are textile shops, variety stores, hardware stores, and quite a few banks. Exploring Denpasar is best done on foot as driving would only be an adventure for someone with a good knowledge of Denpasar's shortcuts and baffling network of one- way roads.

It could be said that Denpasar is a good example of a mid-sized Indonesian city, one that could be found anywhere in the Archipeago. The exception is that almost anywhere you look you can find some attribute of a Hindu temple which is a reminder that this is a Balinese city.

Kumba Sari Market, seen from an ajacent building, Depasar, Bali.

Puputan Square

Denpasar is not famous for its gracious public spaces, but there is one place near the downtown area that does offer its citizens an open a shady place to gather: Puputan Square. It is a grassy field with a monument in the centre and large shady trees around the perimeter. One of South Bali's most important temples is located opposite this field on the north east corner, with the venerable Museum Bali occupying the rest of the eastern border. Puputan is in its glory on Sunday afternoons when families fill the park, together with balloon sellers and food vendors.

The family outings are in absurd contrast to the history of the area around Puputan Square. This field commemorates the massacre committed by the Dutch military on the 20th of September 1906, which effectively ended the long Balinese resistance to Dutch colonization. There were two sites—both royal palaces—for the battles in the Denpasar area that day. The first was located several kilometres north from Puputan Square, at the Puri Agung Denpasar (now called Puri Satria), and the second was at Puri Pemecutan (to the west of Puputan Square). Subsequently, there were several more puputan battles in a number of Balinese kingdoms located mainly in the south central territories of the island. Puputan means 'ending' but implying 'a fight to the death'.

However, the tactics of the Balinese royaly were the same at each battle. When the Dutch troops had massed outside the palace walls and it was certain that the battle was lost, the entire ruling family calmly walked out to the field and either let themselves be killed by Dutch gunfire or killed themselves with their own swords. When the smoke dissipated nobody could be seen alive, except for the Dutch soldiers stunned into silence by the scene. The news of this event reverberated through Europe and it remains today a defining moment in Balinese history.

But today the ghosts of the ruling family and the soldiers are long gone, and this field has been transformed into a marker for the bravery shown by the Balinese royalty, and a place for Denpasar's residents to enjoy themselves.

Denpasar Neighborhoods

Moving away from the city centre the urban spaces become increasingly convoluted and hidden from view. The roads shrink into alleys, and then into narrow sidewalks, and then disappear into the houses and shops of the innermost neighbourhoods. Eventually, you feel that you are travelling through someone's living room and should ask permission to be there.

There is a definite organic feeling in these spaces; it is difficult to imagine that they were formed by a planning committee. And this is not far from the truth. This urban labyrinth originally consisted of separate neighbourhoods that grew closer and closer until they formed a single indistinguishable whole. It is difficult for the outsider to know where the boundaries between these neighbourhoods lie, but the residents themselves know exactly where they are.

Unidentified alley, Denpasar, Bali, 2005.

Driving North through Denpasar approaching the Ayung River bridge.

Pasar Pemecutan is the market for the Pemecutan neighbourhood. Although it is located close to the bustling city centre, it has a village feeling to it.

There are several social norms and ritual requirements concerning the orientation and layout of a Balinese residence, but the decorative embellishments are largely left to the owner's wishes. Making use of this limited freedom of expression is a Denpasar tradition of placing painted concrete statues in front of one's home, school or office. These statues are scattered around town; they are usually well crafted, humorous, and sometimes a bit odd. They are fun to see as you are driving around; taken as a whole they celebrate the tradition of art made by non-artists, without the intervention of professionals.

Above left: a statue by a man who is proud of his employment as Chef De Cuisine at a local resort, and wants the world to know it.

Above right: an unidentified statue in central Denpasar.

Here is a beautiful statue located in front of a maternity hospital in west Denpasar. The artist has fashioned her face with an elongated stylization, and whether intentional or not it gives her a very pensive, far-away expression. In this illustration she is shown freshly painted, but this freshness is quickly lost as the paint soon begins to peel due to the exhaust of the vehicles along this busy road. When the statue starts to look shabby it gets another coat of paint, and depending on the mood of the artist, a different batik pattern on her sarong.

PART 08

MAPPING TODAY,
MAPPING TOMORROW

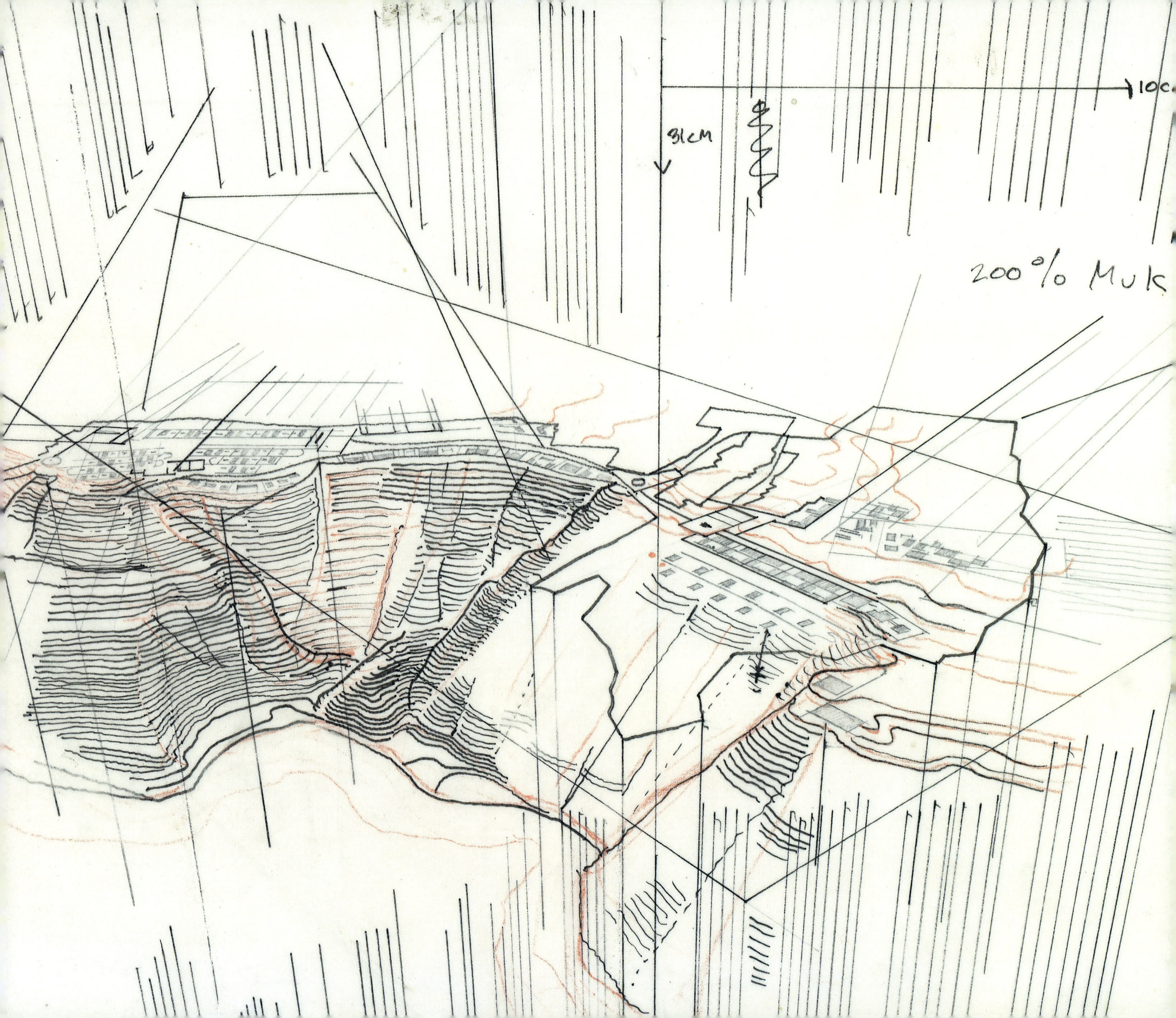

31cm
10c
200% Muk

New Town

If we continue eastward from Gilimanuk through Negara and onwards towards Denpasar we will begin to see the glow of city lights on the horizon. Soon there will be signs of city life, illuminated signs, stoplights, women wearing make-up.

Much of what has been examined in this book is starting to get a slight patina of nostalgia, because these notes have been gathered over a 30 year period. Much of the island indeed had stayed remarkably the same throughout the rapid changes of the last 100 years, but no culture is frozen in time and all the areas of island are now in some form of transition. Nowhere is that more evident than in the urban quarter, and returning to urban Bali after mapping the older parts of the island, we are faced with the challenge of mapping the present and future.

In practice, much of the development in Bali over the last 30 years has been unregulated. To those people who feel that their lives have been unjustly restricted by laws or custom this might seem like a cool breeze of freedom. By cleverly manoeuvering around existing urban zoning codes you could build just about whatever you wanted.

There are strange juxtapositions in urban Bali; huge shop houses plopped down in empty fields, houses built by foreign residents, giant billboards begging for attention. It can all be fun in a darkly humorous sort of way. But cities can't grow uncontrolled beyond a certain density; sooner or later the water will run out, sewage will not just disappear in the ground, conflicting social attitudes will erupt into conflict where different groups of people get pushed together too closely.

To the left, carving a new resort into the steep slope of a deep river valley, East Bali.

Mapping the Future
Seeing and Being Seen

Now that the doors are open and the world has arrived at this small island, the process cannot be undone. Bali cannot become defensive or xenophobic. Up to now the Balinese have been remarkably open-minded and genuinely curious about the life that has arrived on its shores. They could have reacted with fear and anger towards the attitudes and beliefs introduced to their island, some of which are radically different than their own. This is especially true considering that these new ways of living have recently arrived in such a large amount. It is to the credit of the Balinese that they have been able to maintain their curiosity and accommodating spirit, but there is always the possibility of getting too crowded and overwhelmed.

Fortunately, the Balinese have become quite good at picking and choosing from the grand smorgasbord that has arrived at their table. They have not been in a vacuum throughout history, and have demonstrated their skill when incorporating new ideas in their own way. Over the centuries, nothing from the outside has been incorporated in toto, nor have they lost their identity in the swirling waves of South East Asian history. Here are some examples:

When the early Indian merchants visited the coastal settlements of Bali they mainly bought and sold goods, but they also introduced various cultural ideas and religious beliefs. These proved invaluable to the development of early Balinese culture. But again these ideas were adapted selectively, as the Balinese weren't interested in becoming Indian.

Archeological finds in West Bali from about 2,000 years ago include some large stone sarcophagi. This suggests that even though certain Indian customs were being practised at that time, the Indic practice of cremation had yet to be fully accepted. Even today, some of the ancient Balinese funerary practices are still being followed, most notably in the mountain village of Trunyan. One of the most important political imports from India was the image of the king as a god, whose legitimacy was displayed and proven in lavish ceremonies and massive temple complexes. Other cultures in South East Asia also adopted these concepts; their remains are famous today: Ankor Wat, Pagan, Borobudur, Prambanan, even though their respective cultures have all but disappeared.

This concept of the god king proved irresistible to the Balinese leaders at that time, but again they did things in their own way. Instead of carving the universe in stone with the residing king's image enshrined carefully within this microcosmos, the subjects and priests acted out the parts themselves, creating the universe in the ceremonies.

This is one reason for the longevity of this culture: it is not static, it needs to be continually re-enacted. If the earliest Balinese kings had tried to build a massive, Borobudur-style temple complex on Bali they might have killed their own culture. Bali might have become just one more photo op on the way to another ethnic-architectural tourist destination. One of the first Western visitors to Bali was the artist W. O. J. Nieuwenkamp who made several trips here early in the 20th Century. He is remembered today for his disciplined enthusiasm and his skill in preserving his impressions of daily life. These impressions became drawings and paintings and further became prints that he published back in his native Holland. He certainly was not a mercenary, nor dogmatic, he wasn't trying to bring anything or take anything away, but he still had his own agenda. He was looking for a way of life that was 'pristine' and 'unspoiled'. He tended to romanticize the Balinese, their holistic approach to life, their more 'natural' attitude to nudity.

Nieuwenkamp could have spent more time recording the shortcomings of Balinese culture if he had wanted to.

But as he was watching Bali, Bali was watching him. An anonymous local artist carved Nieuwenkamp pedalling around on his bicycle. Presumably, this sculptor wanted to record his impression of this unique figure as clearly as possibly, but the image is unmistakeably Balinese. He is shown with a flower behind his ear and a bicycle with wheels made of lotus flowers.

Throughout their long culture, the Balinese have absorbed and been enriched by those influences they have regarded as useful, disregarded those that seemed destabilizing, and just found humour in those things that seemed irrelevant.

A Paradise Replaced

In recent years there have been several terrorist bombings in Bali which have inflicted terrible suffering; they will be remembered as defining moments in Bali's history. These atrocities have caused a great deal of soul-searching by the Balinese. They have taken a hard look at who they are and what their island is becoming.

There was also a lot of attention from the world towards Bali at the time of these tragedies. Articles appeared in various print media around the world with titles like, "Paradise in Flames" or "Paradise Lost". These articles seem to imply that the bombs ruined something essential to Bali, but this has proved short-sighted and several important things were overlooked in the chaos of that time.

First, there was the incredible amount of self-restraint shown by the Balinese in the aftermath of this violence. There was no mass revenge or vigilante-style mob action taken against the non-Balinese minorities on the island, whether they be other Indonesians or foreigners. In spite of the realization that this tragedy would cause them deep problems for the foreseeable future, the Balinese were able to trust enough in their culture and society to allow their government to administer justice in an orderly manner. They were able to contain their anger and frustration and avoid creating the cycle of violence that has become the pattern that is all too common in the world. The bombers tried to turn Bali into another Sarajevo, Beirut, Dublin, Jerusalem, Somalia, Darfur, Syria or Kashmir, but the Balinese did not permit this to happen, and this is a triumph in itself.

But they were able to go beyond self-restraint. They were able to act, and to act in a way that was truly beautiful. In the aftermath of the first bombings they organized an island-wide religious ceremony for spiritual purification. For people familiar with the Balinese ways, this wasn't surprising because this type of spiritual instinct is deeply ingrained in the Balinese psyche. In fact, the process of organizing and participating in this ceremony appeared to happen automatically. On the day of the ceremony, there just seemed to be a general sense of motion to the beach of people in their ceremonial dress. The depth and maturity of Balinese spirituality allowed them not only too trust in the importance and power of this ceremony, but also to invite people from other religious traditions to join with them and to pray and dress according to their own religious convictions. It's hard to imagine a more powerful example of inclusive spirituality.

Perhaps through the tragedy of the bombings, Bali was able to portray itself to the world for the first time. For even though this island has been known internationally for centuries, it has always been known according to the interests of others. Throughout history, Bali has been marketed in the world by non-Balinese people who wanted something from the island. Originally, it was known as a good place to get slaves, then as an island of savages needing some discipline, and then as a great market to sell opium. The latest image of Bali as a paradise was created by the Dutch in the 1920s for their own reasons and then continued along by the Indonesian Government to this day.

Perhaps the paradise image of Bali has been damaged by the bombs, but how important is paradise to the Balinese anyway? It was never their idea to begin with. Tropical paradises have been trendy for awhile, but the whole idea is a bit silly and very hard to maintain except as a type of cultural caricature. In the end it must be admitted that "paradise" is simply an easy marketing device.

Bali is not heaven and the Balinese are certainly not saints. It is indeed possible to have a bad day on this island. Some people leave here with their backs turned and their middle finger raised. But, fortunately, Bali has something better than paradise and does not need to hold on to outdated and superficial images imported by outsiders. In their response to the bombings, the Balinese showed their true colours to the world for the first time, in their own way and on their own terms. They have shown this island to be a place of a deeply felt self-confidence, both spiritual and cultural, a place where the people are convinced of the power of their own culture. They know clearly who they are, and why they were born. Far from making them fanatic and self-righteous (which is by contrast the symptom of a culture that is in doubt and under siege), this clarity of self allows the Balinese to accept the differences of other people, and to enjoy the spectacle of their guests doing things in their own ways. The Balinese show how a small island can resist being swallowed by a big world by trusting strongly enough in what they have and knowing why it is worth holding on to.

It is in the strength of this trust that an image deeper and more resilient than paradise can be found.

EPILOGUE

During the 34 years this book has been growing and evolving, the life on Bali has continued to change and adapt to the world within and without. The book was more or less finished in the first years of the new millennium, soon after the Bali bombings. At that time these terrorist attacks were the main the main topic of conversation of various groups, both local and international, and it is mentioned in the last section, Bali Replaced. Since then the book has been set aside, waiting for the right combination of conditions to publish it. As a whole it still is a good summary of Balinese life at this time, but should have some supplementary notes to bring it up to date, specifically about the Covid pandemic.

It is difficult to measure the process of the pandemic, and the long-term ramifications to global health, because the results are still pending. But some things can be noted at this point. The effects of Covid and the closed door policy on international tourism has been staggering to the life on Bali. The places that once were full of frenetic activity, were transformed into places of eerie quiet. Some owners of local businesses retreated to secluded corners to wait out the storm. While others urged that this was a perfect time for taking stock and self reflection. Was this the time to re-examine the 'cultural-tourism' of the 1980's?

The local Balinese did what seemed to be the most natural response for them, they returned to their home villages and extended families. These Balinese, who had been working in the tourist trade, brought home new experiences and ways of doing things. Many of them worked in the kitchens of upscale food and beverage operations. Back in the villages they picked up where they left off, preparing food in warungs, but now the familiar dishes have an air of sophistication, and foreign food is now available to those who can afford this minor indulgence. Young men who worked on cruise ships, continued to send back money to their families, and supervise the construction of ponderous trophy houses from a far.

But it would not be accurate to paint a picture of happy villagers, munching on pizza in their lofty concrete palaces. Many people got sick, many people died. The viruses washed over the villages in waves, starting with single families sharing infections, then to neighbors, and finally onward to neighboring villages. The spread of the viral infection was so predictable, it seemed as if a map could be drawn of the viral pathways.

It is hard not to imagine the future defined by these viral battles, organisms great and small spreading around the globe. Each society is responding with its own set of restrictions, laws, and proclamations to deal with an unknown future. Bali has a deeply ingrained understanding of the universe and the human's place in it. This understanding is slightly different from village to village, but as a whole it provides a starting point to deal with an unknown future. And over the centuries this is exactly what they have done.

ACKNOWLEDGEMENTS

This project started in 1986 when I first settled in Indonesia, and has been developing steadily since then. How can I acknowledge all the help and support that people have given me during this time? I think it would be impossible to list them all, but there are several people that need to be mentioned.

I would like to thank Malcom and Jackie Gimse, my two great teachers. In 1980 I joined a student group they led to Asia, introducing me to the wonders and challenges of this region. Most importantly, they taught me how to immerse myself in another culture, how to make a map of a new place.

The work of two scholars has enriched my knowledge of the life of Bali. The first is Adrian Vickers, whose work on Bali's history has given me a working knowledge of the origins of Bali's culture. The other scholar is Steve Lansing whose work on rice field water management has revealed the science that underlies the beauty of the rice fields.

My sincere thanks to George Tahija for letting me use several images from his collection in this book. Taken as a whole, these images help to visualize some of the natural processes that have shaped the Indonesian Archipelago. I appreciate his help and co-operation.

I would like to recall my thanks also to the team at Talisman Publishing, Ian Pringle, Kim Inglis, Stephy Chee, Wong Sze Wey and Janice Ng who not only had faith in this project from the beginning but helped greatly in shaping this beautiful book.

GLOSSARY

Bali Mula. Aboriginal Balinese

Bandesa Clan. Working together with the Pasek Clan (see below), Bandesa helps facilitate the relationships between the commoners and the nobility.

Kaja. In the Balinese system of orientation, kaja is the direction toward Mount Agung, which represents spiritual clarity.

Kangin. East

Kauh. West

Kelod. This is the counter point to Kaja. Kelod is oriented to the sea which represents spiritual dissolution.

Mahabharata. The epic, sprawling, spiritual poem that originated in India and helped build the bedrock of the Hindu religion.

Mount Agung. The tallest mountain in Bali which is considered spiritual to the Balinese.

Pasek Klan. A clan group which over history have acted as intermediary between the kings and the villagers.

Pura. Temple

Pura Besakih. The central temple complex in Bali, where every Balinese Hindu has at least one shrine to pray before

Puri. Palace

Ramayana. Shorter and more focused than the Mahabharata, the Ramayana is built around a single story full of action, heroism, and wisdom.

Siwa. One aspect of the Hindu trinity. He is the God of destruction, who destroys the old to make room for the next cycle of growth.

Subak. The inter village level social group that manages the flow of water through the rice fields.

Wayang Kulit. Shadow puppet theater

IMAGE CREDITS

Studio Satumata is an ad hoc collective of freelance illustrators, up to 15 members, depending on the size of any project undertaken. As the founding member of Studio Satumata, 95% of these illustrations and maps, were created by myself, but credit is also due to several other artists and supporters who contributed their efforts over the 20 years of this project.

There is a lot of preliminary work that needs to be done before the actual paintings begin. Final drawings need to be transferred to the watercolour paper and this kind of work requires patience and careful attention. Two artists helped out with this work: Gede Wijaya and Gusti Ngurah Yasa. Their steady work has gone a long way to make this project successful.

There were two Indonesian artists who need to be thanked for their work on this project. The first is Nengah Nurenten, who has a remarkable ability to describe form. The second is Mubinas Hanafi whose strength is to describe textures and details clearly.

Some additional illustration work was done by Mark Hopkins, especially on the area around Lake Tamblingan on the Bali map and Natalia Granquist did the portraits of four boys and the Sukawana villagers on page 2.

Several images used in this book are my earlier paintings from now in the collection of George Tahja, who very kindly permitted their use in this book.

The same needs to be said to Sheri and Paul Dean, two friends who commissioned from me the large underwater topographic map, a portion of which is seen on pages 24 and 25.

Finally, I would like to thank Eric Oey and Didier Millet, both Singapore-based publishers in supporting my work the years. They both kindly granted permission to reproduce some of my original illustrations from their own output and I wish to acknowledge their generousity.

BIBLIOGRAPHY

Recommended Reading

Style, Grace, and Information in Primitive Art,
From,"A study of Primitive Art" edited by Dr. Anthony Forge,
Oxford University Press
Gregory Bateson

Historical Atlas of Indonesia,
Curzon
Robert Crib

Balinese Traditional Painting,
Exhibition Catalogue,
Australian Museum
Anthony Forge

Negara,
The Theatre State in Nineteenth Century Bali
Princeton University Press
Clifford Geertz

The Painted Alphabet,
Editions Didier Millet
Diana Darling

Mantras to Make Demons into Gods,
Old Javanese Texts and the Balinese Bhutayajnas
Andrea Acri and Michele Stephan

Tales from a Charmed Life,
A Balinese Painter Reminisces
University of Hawaii Press
Hildred Geertz

Images of Power,
Balinese Paintings Made for Gregory Bateson and Margaret Mead
University of Hawaii Press
Hildred Geertz

Kinship in Bali,
University of Chicago Press
Hildred Geertz

The Peoples of Bali,
Blackwell
Angela Hobart,
Urs Ramseyer,
Albert Leemann

The Birthmark,
Memoirs of a Balinese Prince
Periplus
A.A.M. Jelantik

Monumental Bali,
Introduction to Balinese Archeology and Guide to the Monuments
Periplus
A.J. Bernet Kempers

The Shape of Time,
Remarks on the History of Things
Yale University Press
George Kubler

Priests And Programmers,
Techologies of Power in the Engineered Landscape of Bali
J Stephen Lansing

Perfect Order,
Recognizing Complexity in Bali
Princeton University Press
J. Stephen Lansing

A house in Bali,
Tuttle Press
Collin McPhee

Sutasoma,
The Ancient Tale of a Buddha Prince from 14th Century Java
Orchid Press
Kate O' Brien

A Short History of Bali,
Indonesia's Hindu Realm
Talisman
Robert Pringle

The Dark Side of Paradise,
Political Violence in Bali
Cornell University Press
Geoffrey Robinson

Balinese Art,
Paintings and Drawings of Bali, 1800-2010
Tuttle
Adrian Vickers

Bali,
A Paradise Created
Periplus
Adrian Vickers

Journeys of desire,
A study of the Balinese Text Malat
KITLV Press
Adrian Vickers

A statue of Hanoman playing the flute, Banjar Intaran, Sanur, Bali. ink and pencil on paper.

Replacing the thatch on a pavilion, Village Temple, Sebatu, Bali. Ink and pencil on paper.